WILD CHOCOLATE

Truffle Hound: On the Trail of the World's Most Seductive Scent, with Dreamers, Schemers, and Some Extraordinary Dogs

The Essential Oyster: A Salty Appreciation of Taste and Temptation

Apples of Uncommon Character: 123 Heirlooms, Modern Classics, and Little-Known Wonders

Shadows on the Gulf: A Journey Through Our Last Great Wetland

American Terroir: Savoring the Flavors of Our Woods, Waters, and Fields

The Living Shore: Rediscovering a Lost World

Fruitless Fall: The Collapse of the Honey Bee and the Coming Agricultural Crisis

A Geography of Oysters: The Connoisseur's Guide to Oyster Eating in North America

WILD CHOCOLATE

ACROSS THE AMERICAS
IN SEARCH OF CACAO'S SOUL

ROWAN JACOBSEN

BLOOMSBURY PUBLISHING

NEW YORK • LONDON • OXFORD • NEW DELHI • SYDNEY

BLOOMSBURY PUBLISHING
Bloomsbury Publishing Inc.
1385 Broadway, New York, NY 10018, USA

BLOOMSBURY, BLOOMSBURY PUBLISHING, and the Diana
logo are trademarks of Bloomsbury Publishing Plc

First published in the United States 2024

ISBN: HB: 978-1-63973-357-6; EBOOK: 978-1-63973-358-3

LIBRARY OF CONGRESS CATALOGING-IN-PUBLICATION DATA IS AVAILABLE

2 4 6 8 10 9 7 5 3 1

Typeset by Westchester Publishing Services
Printed and bound in the U.S.A.

To find out more about our authors and books visit www.bloomsbury.com
and sign up for our newsletters.

Bloomsbury books may be purchased for business or promotional use.
For information on bulk purchases please contact Macmillan Corporate
and Premium Sales Department at specialmarkets@macmillan.com

CONTENTS

THE TERRAIN OF WILD CHOCOLATE

ATLANTIC
OCEAN

Gulf of
Mexico

MEXICO

Mexico City

Tabasco

Oaxaca

BELIZE

Caribbean Sea

Soconusco

Alta Verapaz

Lacandon Jungle

GUATEMALA

Chuao

VENEZUELA

COLOMBIA

EQUATOR

Amazon

Juruá

Purús

Madeira

B R A Z I L

Marañón

PERU

Mamoré

Tranquilidad

BOLIVIA

São Paulo

PACIFIC
OCEAN

WILD CHOCOLATE

The Soul in the Foam

Oaxaca, Mexico, 2023

Carina Santiago toasts cacao beans on her comal, stirring the almondlike seeds with hardened hands, her long gray hair pulled back in a bun. Flames crackle beneath the hearth. When the clay griddle gets too hot, she switches to a straw brush, watching carefully so the beans don't burn. As they brown, a warm, almost-chocolate scent fills the kitchen.

This is how people have made chocolate for four thousand years, maybe more. You dry the seeds of the cacao tree, which grows in the understory of neotropical rainforests. You toast them, then grind them into a thick, buttery paste that gets mixed into hot water. Although much of the chocolate in the world today gets eaten in solid form, the Indigenous peoples we now call Mesoamericans who invented the process always took it as a drink, and many still do.

Carina sweeps the darkened beans into a clay bowl and pours corn onto the comal, repeating the process. It's a yellow corn grown by her neighbors on the communal lands right here in Teotitlán del Valle, this small Zapotec town a few miles outside Oaxaca City, and it's the only kind she'll use in her chocolate atole.

It's a two-part drink. The base is a simple atole, the corn porridge that has been the daily meal for millions of Mesoamericans for millennia, a sort of liquid tortilla. Carina sweetens hers with a touch of honey, its spicy aroma mingling with the earthy scent of cooked corn as it slowly simmers in a pot over a second fire. It gets topped with the chocolate creation Carina is working on, a merging of the two sacred foods of Mesoamerican culture, the twin poles of the cosmology. Corn, growing in bright sunlit fields, provided the primary sustenance, the clay from which bodies were made. Cacao, from the shaded forest, provided the dark, stimulating drink, the quickening force. Body and blood. Earth and spirit.

"I loved to drink this when I was young," she says, "with my grandma and grandpa. It's a very special memory for me." Later, she learned the recipe from her mother and mother-in-law, who learned it from their moms and abuelitas. "It's been passed down through generations from women I love."

You could trace that line of women back four thousand years, a chain of chocolate reaching to some of Mexico's earliest archaeological sites. It's easy to feel that history in this space, with the clay pots hanging from the adobe walls, the grinding stones, and Carina's bright yellow huipil, woven with patterns that anyone in the valley would immediately recognize as coming from Teotitlán.

Carina lets the corn stay on the comal until its edges begin to blacken and pop, then she sweeps it into its own bowl and adds each ingredient in turn. Wheat—her family's own twist on the classic recipe—then pataxte, a cacao cousin. Carina's daughter ferments its beans in an underground pit for nine months to turn them into excellent foaming agents. Then cinnamon, which gets the lightest toast of all, just a few seconds. Now the room is fragrant with smoke and spice.

I help Carina shell the cacao beans, which are now cool enough to touch, the papery husks sliding off to reveal the shiny beans beneath. Most cacao trees in the world have bitter purple seeds, but in Mexico, traditionalists like Carina insist on the white-beaned cacao known as Criollo, or local. It's nuttier, less bitter, and though now rare, it was the only cacao in Mexico until modern times. It's the flavor that found its way to the heart of the old Maya and Olmec civilizations and that became a global phenomenon. Now it has been replaced almost entirely by what are known as "bulk beans," lacking in character but cheaper to produce—the only chocolate most of us have ever experienced.

Carina places the bowls of ingredients around her metate, the sloped stone grinding table that is the other anchor of the Mesoamerican kitchen. Hers is a hand-me-down from her grandmother. Some metates go back centuries, and are more or less good as new. Carina says that on festival days, the square in Teotitlán will be lined with twenty metates, all the town grannies pounding out chocolate drinks. Everyone has their own family recipe.

She kneels at one end, baguette-shaped stone in hand, and begins to grind the corn into powder, one handful at a time. She lets me take a turn, too, but it's hard. Hard on your back and knees, and hard to learn the fine art of pulling just the right amount of corn under the stone with each motion. In my fumbling hands, our progress slows to molasses. Even in Carina's expert hands, making chocolate atole is a two-hour process.

So why bother? Every town in Oaxaca has mechanical mills that can do the job in seconds.

Sure, Carina admits, it's a labor of love. But that actually *is* the point. She sweeps each powdered ingredient into a wooden bowl at the foot of the metate. The cacao goes on last. And it doesn't turn into powder. As it's crushed under the stone, it transforms into a slick of dark chocolate, the heat of the process melting all that cocoa butter into a glistening paste.

Cacao is ridiculously rich. Coffee beans have about 12 percent fat. Whipping cream has 35 percent. Cacao beans have 55 percent, and these Criollo beans top out around 60. They are butter bombs. That makes them extra delicious, and it also helps the chocolate to defy gravity in the right hands.

Carina scrapes the dark paste into a gourd-shaped clay pot with a spatula. She adds the other ingredients, pours in a little hot water, and begins to whip the heck out of it with a molinillo, a wooden whisk, spinning the handle back and forth between her palms, droplets spattering the sides of the pot. Slowly, the liquid begins to transform, a pillowy foam rising as she twirls, beads of sweat breaking out on her brow, until the whole pot is topped with a cappuccino-colored cloud. "It's a bit delicate," she says, breathing hard. "Not everyone has the gift. You have to handle each ingredient just right, or you won't get the foam."

And the foam is everything, as the ancient Maya and Mexica glyphs attest. Centuries before Italians began steaming milk into a froth to cap their cappuccinos, Mesoamerican cultures were raising the foam on their chocolate, whipping it with sticks or pouring it from on high, one vessel to another, back and forth. In addition to pataxte, some used special flowers or vines to make it extra foamy. In Oaxaca's remote villages and countryside, they still do.

Anyone who's ever obsessed over perfecting their latte hearts can sympathize. "You have to put your love into it," Carina says, filling a small bowl with the hot corn atole and ladling the cool chocolate foam over the top until it's dribbling down the sides like a bubble bath. "When you taste it, you taste the flavors, but you also taste the love."

I'm sure even the ancient Maya enjoyed a little competition over barista bragging rights, but there was more to it, and it gets to the heart of what has brought me to the Valley of Oaxaca in the spring of 2023, raising this quivering cloud to my nose. Chocolate was not drunk lightly. This "drink of the gods," as Carina calls it, was for rituals, festivals, weddings. Every birth was heralded with a round of chocolate. If a man wanted a woman's hand in marriage, he had to bring her family cacao as part of the proposal. And if they accepted, the bride's family provided a good supply of cacao as the dowry, half of which disappeared at the wedding.

Most people who lived in the humid, tropical regions where cacao thrives would have kept a few trees in their forest gardens, plots that had been in the family for generations. In a way, they were part of the family. Festooned in flowers and pods most of the year, cacao trees embodied fertility and renewal. The souls of your ancestors might descend into the underworld upon death, but all this life force was constantly being reborn, and trees, drawing their sustenance from the earth, were its most obvious representation. The stone sarcophagus of Pakal, the great Maya king of Palenque, shows his mother being reborn as a cacao tree. The Maya even buried their dead with ceramic jars of chocolate to take the edge off the journey to the afterlife.

If you lived on the same plot of land as your ancestors, then you were thought to be accompanied by their spirits in tree form.

It's easy to see why the dark liquid made from the seeds of those trees had a special role to play, said to transform your body and mind into a conduit for the generations. This was considered your lifeblood, the most sacred thing you could share with others. When your kids got married, what better way to mark the mixing of two lines than by mixing cacaos? When somebody special visited, what better way to honor them than to whip up a batch of chocolate with a nice frothy head, a cup of you and all that had come before you.

I sip from the bowl, the creamy foam giving way to the invigorating warmth of the honeyed corn. Carina has poured herself into this airy offering, literally elevating it with her effort and skill. She's awakened it.

Chocolate is one of our most complex foods, with hundreds of flavor compounds. It's bitter, sweet, fruity, nutty, and savory all at once. It's also a virtual apothecary of feel-good compounds. It fills the mouth and the mind. Delicious, of course, but that's almost beside the point. The point is the gift.

I can't help thinking how well chocolate is suited to the purpose, this shape-shifter with a knack for capturing its maker's imprint. No wonder it so often plays a role in holidays and gift giving, any moment that needs a little something to make it extra special.

And yet, the chocolate itself is almost never special anymore. Cacao has become one of the most commoditized substances in the world, a $130 billion business built on the backs of fifty million impoverished laborers in the tropics. The link between tree and cup, between maker and taster, has been obscured by a sea of middlemen, and tracing the thread wouldn't make you feel warm and fuzzy. The tree that was once an integral part of the rainforest understory has been a major driver of deforestation.

And the bean once imbued with ceremonial profundity has been transformed into cheap candy by the "capitalist hydra," as Mexico's Zapatistas would put it.

How could it have gone so wrong? How could a substance that was all about heart have become so soulless? And is there still time to right the relationship?

These are the questions I've come to Mexico to explore, as part of a team with the Heirloom Cacao Preservation Fund. They are the questions that have been haunting me for thirteen years, since I unexpectedly got sucked into this world when an unforgettable chocolate bar led me into the Amazon and the unexpected world of wild and heirloom cacao. And what had been a pursuit of flavor became a fascination with this tree's ability to *restore* on all scales: personal, societal, ecological.

Back then, bean-to-bar chocolate was a tiny world known to just a few geeks and pros. While I found it fascinating and beautiful, I wasn't convinced it would ever have much of an impact. It seemed pretty niche. And the empire of industrial cacao seemed so vast.

But I was wrong. Something has shifted in recent years. A rebellion of sorts, led by bean-to-bar chocolate makers, passionate farmers, and pioneers of the ceremonial cacao movement—an alternate universe of people reclaiming cacao. For some of them, flavor is the inspiration. For others, social justice or rainforest restoration. For those who grew up making chocolate by hand in places like Oaxaca, it's also about heritage and tradition. And for those incorporating cacao ceremonies into their spiritual practices, it's about rediscovering chocolate's remarkable ability to polish the mind into a mirror of receptiveness. None of these pursuits are mutually exclusive. Everyone benefits from more meaningful chocolate.

In the following pages, I tell the story of this movement
through the eyes of some remarkable men and women who have
graciously allowed me to share their lives, to tag along on their
adventures through the American tropics. Those journeys have
taken me from the Amazonian basin of Bolivia and Brazil to the
old Maya strongholds of Belize, Guatemala, and Mexico, and
frankly, nothing has gone according to plan. In the rainforest,
things break down. Rivers jump their banks. Plans dissolve like
wet paper in a downpour. Precious bars turn into hot goo. I've
been flayed by ants, menaced by narcotraffickers, crushed by
heat, and stymied by inscrutable directions. I've also been fed
well by countless strangers, transfixed by beauty, and enlightened
by parts of the world rarely seen.

Through it all, I've gained more and more respect for the hero
at the heart of this story, a tree that couldn't be more at home in
this unforgiving environment, or more gifted in providing the
building blocks—food, flavor, intoxication, beauty—from which
culture emerges. To the ancient Maya, it was the most remarkable tree in the universe. I've seen nothing to disagree.

By Any Other Name

The word "cacao," like the tree it names, has been both remarkably resilient and a steady source of confusion. When is the stuff *cacao* and when is it *cocoa*? And is it all the same thing as *chocolate*? And who decided?

The root of the whole thing is the word "kakawa," spoken by the Olmec and related peoples of southern Mexico three to four thousand years ago, right when we find the earliest evidence of ritual chocolate consumption. The Olmec were making and consuming chocolate drinks in ceremonial pottery vessels, and most experts believe they probably started the whole cult we've so enthusiastically inherited. (Though residues of cacao that is more than five thousand years old have been found in pottery in Ecuador, most scholars think those ancient peoples were making booze from the fermented pulp, rather than chocolate from the seeds. But you never know.)

Variations on kakawa were used for cacao seeds and drinks right up to the arrival of the Spanish in the early 1500s. The Maya dropped the final syllable and pronounced it *kakaw*, which the Spanish reproduced using their own spelling conventions as cacao.

The origin of the word "chocolate" is a bit more mystifying. The Nahua people of central Mexico (including the Mexica, formerly referred to as the Aztecs) added their word for water, "atl," to "kakaw" to form the word "kakawatl" for the drink made from cacao beans, literally "cacao water." The Spanish turned this into "chokolatl," and then "chocolate," and so did the Nahuas, but it's unclear if the Spanish got it from the Nahuas or the other way around.

Whatever the case, by the 1600s the convention was to call the beans *cacao* and the drink *chocolate*. When solid eating chocolate arrived with the industrial revolution in the 1800s, and most chocolate production shifted to northern Europe, the convention remained: the stuff you ate was *chocolate*, even though it no longer had any water in it; and the stuff you grew, or bought and sold, was *cacao*, which by then had been smoothed out into *cocoa*, a little easier on English ears. (Adding to the confusion is the odd coincidence that virtually the same sounds also refer to both the bush that is the source of cocaine and the palm nut your piña colada gets served in, both of which often turn up in the same places as cacao.)

We are more or less stuck with those conventions today. Although those who care about authenticity have gone back to using *cacao* for the tree and the bean (*kakawa* would be even better, but it seems like a lot to ask), those who do business in the stuff have steadfastly held on to *cocoa*. Thus we have the World Cocoa Foundation and the Cocoa Board and cocoa powder, the ultimate industrial form of the food. Cocoa is traded on the world commodities exchanges, and *cocoa* is the word used in Africa, where most cacao business is done.

From *chocolate*, of course, comes *chocolatier*, the French word for the artisans who whip the malleable stuff into the confections we know and love. What very few chocolatiers do, however, is make chocolate. They almost all buy blocks of chocolate from large chocolate-making companies, which produce it in massive factories, then melt it down and remold it for their own uses.

That leaves us with the disappointingly pedestrian *chocolate maker* to refer to anyone who actually makes their own chocolate from the beans—not a problem in the days when a handful of multinational behemoths did most of that work, but increasingly awkward since the onset of the bean-to-bar revolution, with thousands of small-scale artisans now doing their own making. One solution comes from Mark Christian, a prominent chocolate philosopher you'll meet very soon. He just calls them "bar smiths."

I

Food of the Gods

Vermont, USA, 2009

For me, this all started with a chocolate bar. It was called Cru Sauvage. It came in a natty green suede box embossed with the silhouette of a feather and stamped with the logo of Felchlin, the century-old Swiss chocolate maker. I slid it open to reveal two thin planks of chocolate wrapped in gold foil, which seemed appropriate. In theory, at least, I was holding chocolate's holy grail.

I'd paid thirteen dollars (plus shipping!) to obtain this precious one hundred grams from Felchlin HQ in the valley of Schwyz. That's a lot today, but back in 2009, it felt insane.

But hey, this was work. I was researching terroir, the way origin of place influences flavor. Why do certain foods from one place taste so distinctive? I'd always loved the romance of terroir, the pleasure of receiving a missive from some far-off place, courtesy of your palate, and by the 2000s I was well versed in the geographies of classic examples like wine, cheese, and oysters.

But chocolate? Although its scientific name is *Theobroma cacao*, "food of the gods"—a nod to its divine status in Meso-american culture—it hadn't been on anyone's short list of great place-based foods. It was just a delicious bulk ingredient to be mixed with sugar and vanilla.

From the culinary heights of the 2020s, it can be hard to remember how drab the world of chocolate was before its creative explosion in the 1990s and 2000s. There was dark chocolate, and there was milk. Dark was what sophisticated Europeans ate. Milk was what everyone else ate. As for gradations of dark, or even the slightest hint of the route one's beans might have taken from forest to bar, well, good luck.

Indeed, like sugar, cacao was a *commodity*, an edible widget filling fields in Africa, freighters in Abidjan, and warehouses in Rotterdam, bought and sold a thousand tons at a time by brokers at computer terminals in London and New York, the price rising and falling at the merciless logic of supply and demand. No one asked about flavor. A bean was a bean. They all sold for the same (absurdly low) price, no questions asked.

But by the 2000s, that was finally starting to change. "Bulk" cacao was still a major commodity, with millions of tons consumed annually, but a tiny category called "specialty cacao" was starting to break out.

It began almost by accident. In 1984, Raymond Bonnat, the third-generation scion of his family's namesake chocolate business—a respected and deeply traditional operation tucked into the town of Voiron in France's Chartreuse Mountains—wanted to do something special to commemorate the company's centennial.

Bonnat had launched in 1884 as a simple chocolatier, but in the twentieth century it distinguished itself as one of France's best chocolate makers. Raymond had spent decades sourcing cacao from all over the world, tracking down the truly exceptional supplies for Bonnat's house blend. At the time, he was one of the few people who thought about origins, who noticed what a difference it made when you got your hands on really beautiful beans, and for the centennial, he decided to give everyone else a taste of that. Bonnat released a collection of eight extra-dark bars, each named for the origin of its cacao: Ivory Coast, Madagascar, Ceylon, Trinidad, Ecuador, and Venezuela's Chuao, Hacienda El Rosario, and Puerto Cabello. He called them the Grand Crus.

Cru is a word from the wine world that refers to a particular vineyard or area. Wines from the best vineyards are often labeled "Grand Cru." By appropriating it for chocolate, Bonnat was implying that chocolate was worthy of the same careful attention to taste and provenance that had long been a hallmark of wine, and that the character of unique beans could be more interesting than the consistency of a blended product.

The move had been intended as a one-off, a fun collector's item for the centennial, but the bars proved so popular that they became a permanent part of the Bonnat line, and they established an important new precedent: people were ready to treat chocolate like wine, to hold it in the same reverence . . . and to pay accordingly.

The Bonnat Grand Crus made such a splash that the idea was quickly copied by Valrhona, Bonnat's larger and more aggressive archrival in Tain l'Hermitage, a mere fifty miles to the west. Valrhona launched its Grand Cru line in 1985 and, with its worldwide distribution, soon eclipsed its competitor and became associated with the concept.

Soon other European chocolate makers joined the arms race, trying to one-up each other with intense bars that showed off the terroir of a particular estate or region. But these makers were only as good as their raw material, and at the time, most of the raw material wasn't very good. Top-end chocolate makers found themselves competing furiously to get their hands on the tiny supply of great beans from which they could coax amazing new flavors. And most of the time, that hunt pointed them in the same direction it would later point me—the Americas.

That was a product of cacao's dark journey from regional delicacy to industrial commodity. And although European planters and businessmen generally get the blame for this, the process had already started before any European ever laid eyes on a cacao bean. Easy to carry, valued by all, and stable for years once dried, the ubiquitous beans were used as currency in many Mesoamerican societies. According to records from the 1500s, one cacao bean could get you a tamale, three an avocado, four a salamander, and eight a night with a prostitute. For the Maya, money literally grew on trees. There were vast cacao orchards in the humid lowlands of Chiapas, small groves in the cenotes of the Yucatán, and a tree or two in the backyard of most everyone who lived in the tropical regions where cacao thrives.

All this was lost on the first known European to encounter the beans, a guy named Christopher Columbus. On August 15, 1502, Columbus's dilapidated Spanish caravel was plying the waters off the coast of Honduras, on his fourth and final voyage to the "New World," when it encountered a hundred-foot-long Maya trading canoe laden with cloth, axes, war clubs, corn beer, and what looked like almonds. Columbus seized some of the cargo, and when a few of those almonds spilled, the Maya merchants leapt after them, in the memorable phrase of Columbus's son Ferdinand, "as if an eye had fallen."

That should have been a sure sign that these mysterious almonds were not your average peanuts, but Columbus missed it. He never followed up, and his voyage ended in tatters in Jamaica a year later.

Europeans would remain clueless to cacao's value until the conquistadores arrived in Tenochtitlán in 1519, seeking gold. The Mexica capital was too high, dry, and cool to grow cacao, but the Mexica ruled the Maya and other Mesoamerican peoples and demanded tribute—a lot of it in the form of cacao beans. When the conquistador chronicler Bernal Díaz del Castillo took part in an elaborate banquet at Montezuma's palace, he watched in astonishment as "50 great jars of prepared good cacao with its foam" were served to the emperor. Later, when the Spanish plundered Montezuma's treasure vaults, they counted *960 million* cacao beans, neatly bundled into 8,000-bean packets. Cacao was the coin of the realm, and the Mexica held the coins.

This time, the Spanish didn't miss the opportunity. They dethroned the Mexica, took over the entire cacao operation in the New World, and began shipping it back home. Chocolate trended with the elites, first in Spain, then the rest of Europe, sweeping London in the 1650s at almost the same moment as coffee and tea. You could find all three stimulants in the city's famous coffeehouses, along with the gossip of the day and a healthy dose of revolutionary fervor. Users noted what the Maya had known for centuries: a shot of chocolate delivered a nice little flush of euphoria. Soon all of Europe was hooked on the stuff, and Spain controlled it. They had found their gold after all.

As demand for chocolate spread worldwide, the orchards of Mesoamerica couldn't keep up. The delicate Criollo cacao of Mesoamerica—the kind I'd enjoyed in Oaxaca with Carina Santiago—was never very hardy, a result of four thousand years of selecting for flavor and pale color at the expense of robustness. Soon new sources of wild cacao were found in the Amazon to supply the market, and these darker varieties turned out to be much more productive and disease-resistant. Eventually, new hybrid varieties were bred that were even more productive. They didn't have the delicious flavor of the old heirloom varieties, but by then cacao was a global commodity. Volume was all that mattered. The new bulk beans were much more profitable, and they were what got planted in all the tropical regions where cacao can grow—especially Africa, which now supplies 75 percent of the world's cacao.

By the end of the twentieth century, 95 percent of world cacao production was low-quality bulk beans. Most of the surviving fine-flavor beans were back in the Americas, remnants of cacao's preindustrial past, where they were still being grown for reasons that had little to do with commerce: tradition, deliciousness, local preference, or simply because they were too remote for Big Chocolate to find and tamper with. For years, most of these fine heirlooms had barely clung to existence. Now, suddenly, chocolate makers were hungry for them.

The iconic story of this era, first reported by Pete Wells in a 2006 *Food & Wine* article titled "The World's Best Chocolate," is the turf war between Valrhona and Amedei, an Italian upstart, for control of Chuao, the grandest of the Grand Crus. Chuao is a fabled valley on the Venezuelan coast, open to the sea but hemmed in on three sides by verdant mountains. It's isolated, accessible only by water, and it's been growing heirloom Venezuelan cacao since the 1600s. When the rest of the cacao world modernized with hybrids and orderly plantations, Chuao never got the memo. The cacao was still shade-grown in the understory, fermented slowly and carefully, and sun-dried by the women of Chuao on the church plaza. And that combination of cacao, climate, and care gave it an explosive flavor with notes of baking spices and blueberry pie. Insiders considered it the best cacao in the world.

By the 1990s, Valrhona had nailed down exclusive access to the entire Chuao supply. And it had become the kingpin of specialty chocolate. It was the most famous company, and Chuao was its flagship bar. But it wasn't paying that much of a premium for Chuao beans, because back then such a practice was unheard of.

Amedei had other ideas. It was founded by Alessio and Cecilia Tessieri, a brother and sister from Tuscany who foresaw that chocolate was following the path of coffee, which was well into its third wave by then. Coffee's first wave was led by commodity brands like Folgers, which simply offered a consistent, though forgettable, product worldwide. Then came second-wave competitors like Starbucks, which improved the roasting process and impressed coffee lovers with darker, more intense blends, but still used fairly cheap ingredients. That led to the third wave of coffee, which focused on beans from unique locations and the singular flavors they could produce.

Alessio Tessieri recognized that the same thing was now happening with chocolate, and he spent the 1990s traversing Latin America, meeting with farmers, tasting beans, forging relationships, learning where to find the most interesting varieties, and tweaking fermentation protocols to coax the most amazing flavors from them. And that work paid off. By the

2000s, Amedei was making some of the most coveted single-origin chocolate bars in the world.

But Alessio was dead-set on securing the most prized beans of all: Chuao. According to Wells, this was because he had a grudge against Valrhona. When he and his sister, Cecilia, started their company as a high-end confectioner in 1990, they had hoped to source their chocolate from Valrhona, but the Italians were turned away. "The French wouldn't even negotiate," Wells wrote. "According to Cecilia, they were told that Italy wasn't evolved enough to appreciate such extraordinary chocolate. It was a personal slight, a national insult, a call to arms. 'Right then and there,' Cecilia would later say, 'it was war.'"

And in that war, Chuao was the ultimate prize. Alessio worked on Chuao's farmers for years, visiting the cooperative regularly, slowly earning trust on the ground. He bought new farming equipment for the cooperative. He even bought new uniforms for the baseball team.

But what really made the difference was cold, hard cash. He offered to triple the price Valrhona was paying, and to pay up front. And it worked. In 2004, the coup was complete. The Chuao cooperative sent registered letters to Valrhona and other chocolate makers announcing that all its beans would be going to Amedei, and only Amedei had the right to use its name.

The move vaulted Amedei into the upper echelon of chocolate luminaries. But even more than that, it burnished Chuao's luster and made it clear how valuable a great origin could be.

In Europe, at least. One startling thing about Wells's 2006 story is how he felt it necessary to explain all these concepts to Americans. Wells admitted that "Amedei is sold in only a handful of stores in the U.S., and . . . few Americans have heard of it." As for the notion that great cacao beans could make a big difference in the chocolate and might be coveted—that was all news in the United States.

But Americans caught on fast. A few tastemakers were already working on it. One of them was Matt Caputo, a young importer who would become a driving force in the fight to save heirloom cacao.

Matt is a toned, dark-haired workaholic with a straightforward manner and a Midwesty demeanor. He grew up in Salt Lake City in the 1990s, working alongside his dad, Tony, at Caputo's, the deli Tony had started. By the early 2000s, Caputo's had expanded from a simple deli into the go-to spot in Salt Lake for specialty foods of all kinds. It was famous for things like cheeses and cured meats, which Matt curated, and he believed his chocolate section was equally worthy.

At the time, "gourmet" chocolate in the United States meant bars with high cacao content and endangered animals on the label, all made in big factories with cheap industrial chocolate. These were the bars of America's second wave of chocolate, and they were driven as much by health trends as by flavor. The media had recently anointed chocolate as the newest superfood, packed with protective antioxidants, and the rush was on to find bars with higher cacao content and less sugar. Whereas a few years earlier it had been nearly impossible to find a chocolate with more than 50 percent cacao content, suddenly bars were appearing with 60, 65, 70, even 80 percent cacao. Like a burnt Starbucks dark roast, these bars were intense. They just weren't very good.

And Caputo's selection was no better. One day, however, a friend of Matt's who'd spent time in Europe explained that a new world of bars was appearing—bars made with better ingredients and better technique. And Caputo's was behind the curve.

"And I didn't like that," Matt told me. His reputation as a taste leader was on the line. He knew he needed to up his game, so he embarked on a pilgrimage to the one place where he might find enlightenment: the Fancy Foods Show in New York City.

Matt headed straight for the Italian pavilion, because he'd heard they were making the best chocolate at the time. He immediately felt out of place. "Man, those Italians wear suits so well!" he recalled with an embarrassed laugh. "And here I am, this punk deli kid from Salt Lake in a T-shirt. And I would just stand at the counters, patiently waiting for someone to talk to me. And no one would ever talk to me."

Finally, a woman at one of the Italian booths took pity on the earnest kid in the T-shirt. She sat him down at a table and put two chocolates in front of him. "She said, I'm gonna let you taste these chocolates. They only have two ingredients: cacao beans and sugar. They're all made on the same equipment with the same recipe. The only difference is where the beans come from."

The first was from Ecuador. The woman told him to expect an earthy, nutty flavor with very little acidity. "And so I tasted it, and it really did taste like that! And I just thought, 'Wow, that's uncanny!'"

The second sample was from the Sambirano valley of Madagascar. "And she said that because of the terroir, it's going to taste like tart fruit, like raspberries and citrus . . . And I prepared myself for very slight differences . . . And I popped it in my mouth, and I was hit with this fresh fruit! It tasted like raspberries and citrus! My mind was swimming. I could feel myself falling down the rabbit hole. This had more terroir, more of a taste of place, than anything I'd ever experienced. It didn't taste like candy. It tasted like the food of the gods!"

Matt headed home determined to get Caputo's up to speed. When he discovered that half the brands he wanted to carry weren't available in the States, he launched his own importing and distribution company, A Priori Specialty Food, to bring them in, and he tricked out Caputo's selection with his favorites. Amedei and Domori from Italy. Michel Cluizel, Bonnat, Valrhona, and Pralus from France. Felchlin from Switzerland. And Scharffen Berger, the only serious U.S. contender at the time.

That kind of transformation was happening in good chocolate stores all over the United States in the late 2000s. Chocolate could be an experience and people were eager to have it, to taste their way through Venezuela and Ecuador and the Sambirano valley.

And so was I. To be honest, I hadn't expected much from my chocolate quest. A childhood of bad mass-market chocolate had left me indifferent to the stuff. (If you haven't recently tasted a regular old Hershey bar, you might be shocked at how weird it is. It tastes less like chocolate than like a vanilla-scented candle recovered from a warehouse after an electrical fire.) And sure, in 2009 there were still plenty of bad bars out there. But the more I tasted, the more I came across fragrant treasures that bore no resemblance to the crappy chocolate of my youth. And the more I tasted well-made bars from the handful of craft chocolate makers who were rediscovering heirloom varieties and treating them with care, the more I became convinced that chocolate was becoming something new—or maybe returning to something very old.

Like the best wines, these next-level chocolates packed complicated and extraordinary flavors into a package that unfolded and changed over time. They were completely captivating, and they rewarded attention and thought in the same way that wine did. But the most exciting part to me was that, unlike wine, the territory hadn't been mapped to death. There was no appellation system for chocolate. There were no Master Sommeliers. There weren't even any good guidebooks, just a subculture of choconerds debating the merits of various offerings in online forums.

As I snooped around the forums, looking for clues, one mysterious bar kept popping up. Cru Sauvage. Felchlin seemed to be one-upping its Grand Cru rivals Bonnat and Valrhona, claiming that this was the first bar made entirely with *wild* cacao, from the Bolivian Amazon. Other experts said that was impossible. Cacao was domesticated in Central America thousands of years ago. Wild cacao? A myth. A marketing gimmick. Disappeared centuries ago. And it certainly wouldn't be coming from Bolivia, a country that had never been a source of fine cacao.

Whatever its provenance, the few people who had managed to get their hands on a bar were united in their adulation. Seventypercent listed it as one of the top ten bars *of all time*. TheChocolateLife, the most elaborate of the sites, said it was the real deal. Mark Christian, a particularly obsessive and eloquent choconerd, whose reviews could make or break a bar, went even further. "An incunabulum of how it might have been," he wrote. "Unless you're the age of Methusaleh or old as diamonds, you've probably had nothing like it." His only quibble was that, considering the incredible smoothness of the flavor, Felchlin could have pushed the cacao content higher. "With such a gentle disposition, this bean's tolerance could handle more than the current 68% cacao content; perhaps well into the mid-to-upper 70 percentile to crown it the greatest bar on Earth."

Incunabulum. That was an interesting word choice. It refers to the very earliest printed books, before the printing press jump-started mainstream culture. Was this bar the key to some sort of prelapsarian chocolatey paradise? There was only one way to find out. I ordered one. And here it was. I peeled back the foil, snapped off a shard, placed it on my tongue, and closed my eyes.

2

The Call of the Wild

Beni, Bolivia, 2010

For all its amazing flavor, chocolate's real superpower is its plasticity. Cocoa butter, the unique fat that composes about half of a dry cacao bean, has an unusually sharp melting point that falls just above room temperature. That's what allows chocolatiers to work their magic, transforming the solid mass to liquid with a nudge of heat, then swirling and enrobing to their heart's content before letting the edible art firm up again, awaiting suitors.

But the most miraculous part is what happens when that suitor arrives. Because chocolate's melting point falls between room and body temperature, it goes beautifully fluid on the tongue, releasing a bevy of aromatic molecules.

And that was the case with this Cru Sauvage. It melted like silk. The flavor dove into a deep, dark place, and then, just when I thought I had a handle on it, the bottom fell out and it dove some more. The aroma was rich and spiced, a tobacco barn in August.

But beyond the physical experience, there was something . . . metaphysical. I felt *good*. There was a flash of bliss, a momentary bolstering, as if the gods had my back. I felt a wormhole open. And it led straight to the Amazon.

Was it really possible that such excellent stuff had been overlooked for centuries? And if it was truly wild, why would it taste so refined? For all the ink spilled on the glories of foraged ingredients, wild plants are rarely as tasty as their domestic kin. Wild tomatoes are the size of pinky nails. Wild corn is nearly inedible. It usually takes centuries of selection to transform a wild plant into a friendly food. Why would cacao be any different?

I was skeptical. But that didn't make the mystery any less alluring. So when the good feeling began to subside, I opened my eyes and tracked down the man responsible for the bar.

His name was Volker Lehmann. I'd gleaned the basic elements of his story from a few tidbits online. Volker was a German agroforestry expert who'd been working in the Amazon for twenty years, trying to develop sustainable economies. He'd come to Felchlin with samples of the cacao beans he claimed he was finding wild in Bolivia. They were weird; half the size of normal beans; so small they wouldn't even work on Felchlin's equipment. But the flavor? Phenomenal. So Felchlin's engineers rejiggered some old equipment and made it work. Volker shipped them the beans, and they cranked out the Cru Sauvage.

When I made contact with Volker via Skype, he said he'd struggled for years to get a good chocolate maker interested.

"They don't even know Bolivia has cacao," he told me in frustration. "They think we make llamas."

By then I'd done enough homework to know that it was at least theoretically possible for Bolivia to have wild cacao. True, Bolivia is best known for its Andean mountains and cultures, La Paz and Lake Titicaca, but its lowlands include a vast stretch of Amazonia known as the Beni, and that was where Volker was getting his beans. That put him just a few hundred miles from the cradle of cacao, the soupy section of the Upper Amazon where Brazil, Colombia, Ecuador, and Peru come together.

Few people in the chocolate industry understood this. Because chocolate reached its cultural zenith under the Maya, who introduced it to the rest of the world, people long assumed that *Theobroma cacao* was native to Mesoamerica. In the 2000s, advances in genetic sequencing allowed scientists to trace its origin back to the Amazon (see "Interlude: First Families" for more on this), but until recently, only a few scientists and history buffs understood this. People who worked in chocolate simply knew that cacao came from West African farms, if they thought about it at all. Most of them had never seen a cacao tree. As far as they knew, it came from a warehouse.

When I told Volker that my sources said there was no such thing as wild cacao, he just laughed. They know nothing, he said. Come see for yourself.

In fact, he was about to head deep into the jungle on a scouting mission. Local traders he worked with had told him that whole forests of wild cacao lay far up the Mamoré River, ripe for the picking. An Indigenous group called the Yurucaré that lived in the area sometimes harvested the pods and sold them on a small scale. The current prices were so low that they rarely bothered anymore, but their chief had expressed interest in working with Volker to raise prices and bring some sustainable income to the Yurucaré. So Volker needed to show face, assess the situation, and see if something could be worked out. Why not come along?

Catnip, obviously. He had me at "jungle."

And that was how, in March 2010, I found myself circling the Amazon in a small plane, looking desperately for a place to land.

Simply getting to the Beni was not for the faint of heart. For me, it involved a flight to Miami and a sleepless red-eye to Santa Cruz de la Sierra, the big Bolivian city in the lowlands. There, I met Volker. Intense guy, fifty-three, thin and balding, with a German exactitude and a wry humor that seemed to be some sort of coping mechanism for operating in an environment that ate exactitude for lunch. "Many people have lost their fortunes here," he told me. "There's no *Bolivia for Dummies*." He mentioned that one of his favorite movies was *The Mosquito Coast*, about an eccentric American inventor who renounces consumerism and moves his family to the Central American jungle.

"Doesn't that guy die?" I asked. Volker just shrugged. He had a wife and two young daughters in Santa Cruz, where he spent the offseason, but so far they had opted to take no part in his jungle existence.

We hopped a sixteen-seat plane to Trinidad, a swampy town with frogs trilling in the gutters. It was early March, the tail end of the rainy season. The rivers had risen thirty feet and spilled across the forests. Trees stood in six feet of water. Piranhas had abandoned the river channels for better hunting in the woods.

Trinidad was basically an overgrown trading post where the Mamoré River met the rudimentary road system. Traders still plied the river as they had for centuries, bartering with the forest dwellers for cacao, bananas, skins, anything that could be sold back in Trinidad. The only difference was that they'd swapped their paddles for outboard motors with propellers at the end of eight-foot shafts that can be raised for navigating shallows. These are ubiquitous in the Amazon, and they make it look like everyone has weed whackers strapped to their sterns. They call them pika-pikas, for the sound.

Traveling upriver to Yurucaré territory would have taken us days, so we hired a bush pilot to fly us into the zone and drop us near the river, where a trader named Aurelio would meet us in his dugout.

For an hour, we crossed an unbroken carpet of green. Cocoa-colored rivers snaked through the flats. Light reflected back at us from beneath the tree canopy, a sign of just how flooded the forest was. The jungle was steaming, mist rising to form immense thunderheads, and the thunderheads were dropping ropes of black rain back to earth. It felt like we were a tiny submarine threading our way between monstrous jellyfish above and a hungry mat of green anemones below.

As we approached the drop site, our pilot, a mustachioed man of few words, pointed to the ground and shook his head in dismay. I could see a long green rectangle cut from the forest, near a little cabin on a river. Our landing strip. But from the way light bounced off the strip, I could tell it was half underwater.

The pilot shook his head again and veered off, searching for alternatives. I was surprised that here, in the remotest Amazon, we'd have any, but I shouldn't have been. Later, I'd learn that the Beni is littered with landing strips because it's the heart of the cocaine flyway that moves drugs from Bolivia, Peru, and Colombia to the markets of Brazil and beyond.

Cocaine starts as coca, a bush that grows in the foothills of the Andes. The plant has always been the sacred stimulant of Andean cultures, made into tea or chewed in a big wad. It's legal and ubiquitous in Bolivia, and pretty mild. But pure cocaine can also be extracted from the leaves using chemicals and solvents.

And most of that work gets done in the Beni, away from prying eyes. Boatloads of dried coca leaves, along with barrels of aviation gas, are shipped downstream from coca-growing regions on the Mamoré and other rivers, then refined into cocaine in riverside labs tucked into the jungle. Then planes swoop in, pick up the drugs, refuel, and continue on to Brazil. It's a lucrative business, and a fiercely defended one. More than one person has been gunned down when they accidentally stumbled onto a cocaine lab.

The other landing strips we found looked even worse than the first. The pilot kept circling back to our original option, as if he were trying to psych himself up. We punched through a storm, and water came spitting through the vents of the plane. I shot a questioning glance at the pilot, but he just waved me off.

When to worry? For that, I was counting on Volker, who seemed unfazed in the seat behind me. He'd been navigating this environment for twenty years, after all. But the *Mosquito Coast* thing kept nagging at me, and I began to fear that his appetite for doom was considerably higher than mine.

Without warning, the pilot banked the plane hard toward that original strip. The ground rose fast, the overgrown brush on the runway clearly visible. I barely had time to grab the emergency strap and brace for impact before we thunked into the brush, the sickly shriek of vegetation raking the metal sides of the plane, and came to a stop a few feet from the river.

My emotions boomeranged back to elation. I flashed the pilot an earnest thumbs-up. He shrugged in disregard. I grabbed my pack and hopped out. Volker climbed out behind me.

And just like that, first time in the Amazon. Flocks of parrots chittered through the towering canopy. Thick vines dropped to the floor a hundred feet below. I breathed the thick green air. For a moment, my *Mosquito Coast* premonitions morphed into *African Queen* fantasies of tooling downriver to take part in riotous chocolate ceremonies, rivers of molten deliciousness pouring down my chin.

And then four guys with rifles stepped out of the cabin and came our way, and my chocolate fantasies melted. We held our hands at our sides in a noncommittal way, trying to telegraph our nonthreatening nature. The guys had three-day stubble and sweat-stained shirts, and they seemed unnerved by our presence, which rattled me all the more. Sure enough, they said they were watching the place for their boss, a Colombian man, and we had just landed on his private strip without permission. And he wouldn't be happy about that.

And let's be honest, neither was I. How was it possible that I'd been in the Amazon all of five minutes and I was already on crisis number two? My fate was in the hands of a guy I'd literally met yesterday, and I was beginning to wonder if this was just how life went in the chocolate trade: beauty and darkness, hopelessly entangled. That would turn out to be one of the few things I got right.

3

The Golden Pod

Beni, Bolivia, 1991–95

I n Volker Lehmann's twenty years in the neotropics, he had
indeed seen a ton of darkness to go with the beauty, but it
never broke the spell for him. He'd been smitten since day one,
and it all stemmed from growing up in postwar Germany.

His father had been a soldier in the German army who barely
survived the war. He spent the rest of his life working double
shifts in the coal mines, the only job available. In this grim existence, his solace was gardening, and that was Volker's best
chance to spend some time with him. "In the beginning, I didn't
like it much," he told me during one of our many downtimes in
the jungle. "I had to help a lot, pulling out the weeds. And sometimes I missed and pulled out a carrot. But, you know, all part
of the education." Eventually, he fell in love with the magic of
making food out of soil, water, and air.

But he never liked the German climate, so after high school,
he took a trip to Latin America. And compared with the gray

horizons of postwar Germany, it was like stepping into Oz. "I was intrigued by the culture," he remembered. "The climate, the music, the food. The way the people meet in the mornings and go out into the fields and harvest and laugh. The way they live together and share."

Most of all, he was astonished by the sheer fecundity of the tropics. He came home and told his parents he was going to get a degree in tropical agriculture. They were horrified. They'd been hoping he'd be a banker. But he stuck to his guns, got his degree, and in the 1980s joined the German Volunteer Service, the German equivalent of the Peace Corps, working on sustainable agriculture initiatives in the neotropics.

In 1991, he came to Bolivia for a six-month stint and discovered a living time capsule. In terms of development, Bolivia was decades behind its neighbors, and the Beni was bringing up the rear, a Florida-sized quilt of rainforest and Everglades-like grasslands. Caimans and capybaras splashed through the marshes. Jaguars prowled the woods. Giant storks wheeled overhead. Indigenous groups still hunted and gathered in the forest.

But that was changing. People from overcrowded cities in the Andes were moving to the region and clearing forest for farming. There were clashes with a local Indigenous group called the Chimané. Some had turned deadly. In response, the Chimané were fading deeper into the jungle.

There was a pattern to the clearing. The settlers would slash and burn the forest, then grow rice on the land. But rice exhausts the soil within a couple of years, so they would turn that land over to cattle grazing and slash new forest for rice. And so the agricultural front kept chewing up the forest.

And that was where Volker came in. His job for the Volunteer Service was to figure out a system of sustainable agroforestry—tree permaculture—that could replace the rice and cattle. "Because if you plant trees," he explained to me, "then you stay with your trees. That's the trick."

But which trees? He checked out bananas, plantains, citrus, and the same hybrid cacao that was being grown all over the world. He was especially interested in native plants that might be well adapted to the local climate, so he also looked at rubber trees and Brazil nuts and acai.

But these were all well-known options. Volker was especially curious about the unknown. After all, the Amazon was Nature's apothecary, filled with plants whose potential for food and medicine had barely been tapped. He didn't know where to start, but he knew who to ask. The Chimané knew all the plants in the forest.

He chatted with everyone he came across in the frontier town where he was based. One tree kept coming up: wild cacao. There were patches of it in the forest. The Chimané didn't make chocolate with it, they just used it like a regular fruit, but they knew where to find it.

Volker was intrigued. *Wild* cacao? He'd never heard of such a thing. And fortunately for him, at the time he didn't know enough about the cacao trade to know that experts would have laughed at the notion. So he persisted. Who could show it to him?

Eventually, he learned of an old Chimané woman near the town where he was based who still lived as a hunter-gatherer, traveling seasonally. One day he made the trek into the forest and tracked her down.

She was tiny, with a huge nest of gray hair and a dress made of vines. Her home was a thatch tent. She barely spoke a word of Spanish, but when he mentioned cacao, she nodded and set off through the woods at a brisk pace. He scrambled after her.

As he walked behind, a tiny face popped out of her nest of hair and began chattering at him. It was a miniature monkey, with a furry mustache and a long tail with a bushy tip. Volker was transfixed. He'd seen these little monkeys being kept as pets, but he'd never seen one living in somebody's hair before.

Eventually, the old woman stopped beside a small tree. Golden pods dangled from its limbs and even directly from its trunk. She pointed, jerked a pod off the tree, and held it out to him. "Cacao!" she said.

He took the pod from her. It was tiny, compared with the farmed cacao he knew, but it sure looked like the same plant. How had he never seen or even heard of this fruit before? The monkey chattered insistently at him. It felt like the Amazon was trying to tell him something.

But what? Was this cacao any good? Was it like regular cacao? How much of it was there? Could it ever be cultivated in a farm setting? There were too many questions to make it anything more than a long-shot candidate, but it was a tantalizing one, definitely worth checking out.

Which is what he said in the report he submitted to the German Volunteer Service when his six-month stint in Bolivia ended. On the short list of trees that might work for agroforestry in the Beni, he included wild cacao as an outlier. No idea if it could ever generate any income, he conceded, but it's already here. Somebody should follow up.

And then he tucked wild cacao away in a back corner of his mind. The mystique of the tree stayed with him, but it would be seven years before he could act on the impulse. In between, his

attention would be monopolized by another native plant that had
already proven its market viability—and gained America's wrath.

By 1995, Bolivia's coca farmers had been sucked deep into the
drug wars. Cocaine production had long been centered in
Colombia, but a U.S.-led crackdown in the 1980s had shifted the
action. "Bolivia was the expansion project for the Colombians,"
Volker explained to me. "First they moved into Peru, and then
that wasn't enough, so they moved over to Bolivia." Volker
returned to Bolivia with a new assignment from the German
government: convince Bolivia's coca farmers to grow something
else instead.

Volker wound up in Santa Cruz de la Sierra, the hub of the
lowlands. "Santa Cruz was like Carnival in Rio 24/7," he said.
"A lot of drugs." Most of the action was in the Beni, a smuggler's paradise of barely populated grasslands and cattle ranches
the size of national parks. The only way to get around the
ranches was by small plane, so the Beni was full of landing
strips. And usually the only eyes on you were the cows' and the
crocodiles'.

The smugglers and the ranchers quickly bonded over their
mutual love of guns, planes, open spaces, and libertarianism, and
soon Bolivia's ranchers were saddle-deep in the drug business.
The ranchers helped the smugglers transport their packages,
and the more successful smugglers bought their own ranches.
Cattle turned out to be a great way to launder drug money.

A small town in the Beni called Santa Ana de Yucuma
became the center of the action, and everybody knew it. It was
the height of the drug wars, when the U.S. Drug Enforcement

Agency was aggressively expanding its efforts to nip cocaine production at the source, and on the night of June 28, 1991, it pounced. Dozens of helicopters carrying hundreds of antidrug agents swooped down on Santa Ana de Yucuma. The agents destroyed fifteen cocaine labs hidden in the little town and confiscated dozens of planes, along with hundreds of kilos of coke. But they met stiff resistance from the townspeople, who stormed the airport and surrounded the helicopters, chanting "Kill the Yankees!" The villagers were repelled with tear gas, which only hardened their feelings.

After that, many Bolivians came to resent the U.S. meddling in their country. It felt increasingly like an occupation. Herbicides in the coca fields. Farmers thrown in jail. When an undercover DEA agent's gun accidentally went off in a Santa Cruz nightclub and shot a local man, hatred of the Americans began to boil over.

The German government was also active in Bolivia. Germany has long been the second-largest source of foreign aid in the world, after the United States, and Germany had maintained a strong relationship with South America since the early 1800s. With tensions spiraling, the German government introduced a softer approach, the carrot instead of the stick: pay the farmers to try alternative crops. And Volker was their point person.

He worked with the farmers on lots of different options. Bananas, pineapple, hearts of palm. None of the alternative crops sold for nearly as much money as coca, but he liked the work. He learned a lot about Bolivian culture, living his teenage dream of working with everyone in the fields. He was making friends all over, partying in discotheques with dudes who just had to be smugglers.

I asked him if that had ever made him nervous, but Volker said no. "You know, you'd sit next to one, and he'd say, 'Oh, where you come from?' He wants to know who you are, if you're DEA. And then he puts a bottle of whiskey into you, and you both start singing, and then he says, 'Oh, this guy is harmless!'"

And he drank chocolate with everyone. Since his fateful meeting with the Chimané woman years earlier, he'd seen rustic chocolate patties for sale in the markets around Bolivia. It was an old Bolivian tradition, just like in Mexico. By the 1990s, it was already pretty much a thing for old-timers—even in Bolivia, the younger generation was abandoning the local discs in favor of Swiss Miss—but he was hanging out with a fair number of old-timers, and they reliably offered a cup of chocolate.

To his astonishment, he learned that it was being made with wild cacao. It was a cottage industry in Bolivia, collected by campesinos in the Beni and produced by a handful of tiny factories, strictly for domestic consumption. So you could actually make chocolate from these wild trees, and to Volker's amazement, there seemed to be enough to supply the domestic market.

You'd think that would have stoked Volker's agroforestry fantasies, but he still didn't take the cacao too seriously for one important reason: the chocolate sucked. It had a harsh, burnt-rubber flavor, sometimes bordering on blue cheese, and a granular texture. None of this fazed the old-timers, who drank it sweet as syrup, but to Volker's taste, the stuff had no potential.

Eventually, he soured on the coca work, too. It felt pointless. The program triggered a wave of new coca planting across Bolivia, as farmers rushed to start growing it so the Germans would pay them to stop. Even the farmers who switched to alternative crops just planted coca elsewhere. Everything seemed to result in more forest clearing.

So he quit. He wanted to do *real* agroforestry, finding ways for people who lived in the rainforest to earn an income from living trees, rather than dead ones. And just in time, the mother of all opportunities came along . . . right in the Beni, of all places.

First Families

Like wine grapes, cacao beans come in different varieties, each with its own characteristic appearance, tendencies, and flavor. And for both wine and chocolate, a big part of understanding the flavorscape is knowing a little about these varieties.

Until the twenty-first century, the cacao categories were very simple—too simple, as it turned out. Everything was divided into three varieties. First among them was Criollo, the great cacao of Mesoamerica. The cacao with which chocolate was invented, the only game in town throughout Central America and Mexico, Criollo had the chocolate market to itself until the 1600s, when diseases ravaged it, and demand began to outstrip supply.

To make up the difference, cacao was sourced from South America, where it grew wild in the Amazon and was being farmed near the coasts. But this foreign, or forastero, cacao didn't have Criollo's delicate nature, which was the result of thousands of years of selection. It was more robust, bitter, and astringent, and the people in Mesoamerica didn't like it. They stuck with their beloved Criollo, if they had any choice. Forastero came to be known as "the chocolate of the poor," foisted on those who couldn't afford Criollo or who didn't know any better, which increasingly included the exploding European market.

In addition to Criollo and forastero, a third category was added in the 1700s, when yet another disease decimated the Criollo groves and people turned to a new hybrid from Trinidad, known as Trinitario, which combined some of the fine flavor of Criollo with the hardiness of forastero.

And that was it for centuries. Fine chocolate came from Criollo or Trinitario beans, which accounted for a tiny percentage of cacao production. The rest came from forastero beans, the "bulk" cacao that dominated world production.

Because the culture of chocolate had come from Mesoamerica, many experts assumed that was where the tree had originated. Right through the twentieth century, it was an open question. Perhaps people had carried cacao from Mesoamerica to South America? Or maybe Criollo was native to Mesoamerica and forastero to South America?

But in the 2000s, new technology made it possible to affordably sequence the genomes of thousands of cacao cultivars and come up with a new family tree. That work was released in 2008 by Juan Carlos Motamayor, then at the U.S. Department of Agriculture's Agricultural Research Service, and his colleagues, and it transformed the world's understanding of cacao origins.

Motamayor found that all modern cacao could be traced back to ten original families or clusters that had evolved in the Upper Amazon. There the tree must have existed for millennia, a snack for monkeys and parrots, until humans came along ten thousand years ago and discovered the delicious pulp inside the pods, sweet as soursop yet tart as lemonade, so refreshing in the thick heat of the jungle. The seeds were bitter, so those you spat out.

At some point, somebody realized that if you filled a container with the seedy pulp and waited a few days, the pulp would liquefy and ferment into delightfully fizzy cacao wine. And it was probably as a source of fermentable sugars that cacao spread from its Upper Amazon home to the other tropical parts of South America.

Of those original ten families, only one, Criollo, spread north into Mesoamerica. Criollo is also the variety with the palest seeds and least bitterness. Motamayor found that Criollo's genetic diversity was much narrower than the others'—a sign of domestication. At some stage of its journey north, somebody had figured out that cacao seeds that had been pickled in the alcohol and acids of the fermenting pulp didn't taste so harsh anymore. In fact, if you dried and toasted them, they were pretty great. Criollo and Mesoamerica invented chocolate together, and then the practice spread back to the Amazon.

Motamayor named the ten original varieties Amelonado, Contamana, Criollo, Curaray, Guiana, Iquitos, Marañón, Nacional, Nanay, and Purús. Each was named for a geographical feature near the area where it evolved (such as the Purús River in Brazil, or the city of Iquitos in Peru), except for Amelonado, Criollo, and Nacional, which were already known by historical names. Amelonado, a variety from eastern Brazil named for its melon-shaped pods, is the type of forastero that came to dominate the world supply, thanks to its high-yielding nature. Almost all the cacao grown in Africa has an Amelonado background, and Amelonado's earthy, fudgy, astringent flavor has come to define what we think of as the taste of chocolate. In contrast, Nacional, the celebrated cacao of Ecuador, has an elegant, jasmine-like fragrance that has little in common with conventional chocolate. Most of these families exist in pure form only in small numbers in the wild and have never been made into chocolate on their own. Instead, their DNA turns up in the mix of many different cacao cultivars.

Since Motamayor's landmark report, two additional cacao families that are remarkably distinct from the rest, in terms of both genetics and flavor, have been identified: Beniano, the wild cacao of Bolivia's Beni region, and Juruá, the wild cacao of Brazil's Juruá River. They are two of the stars of this book.

And there are more to be found. In all likelihood, the Amazon and other remote corners of Latin America harbor other unique families of cacao waiting for their big moment. The search continues.

FIRST FAMILIES

ATLANTIC
OCEAN

Gulf of
Mexico

MEXICO

BELIZE

Caribbean Sea

GUATEMALA

VENEZUELA

COLOMBIA

EQUATOR

Amazon

Juruá

Purús

Madeira

PERU

Marañón

Mamoré

BRAZIL

BOLIVIA

PACIFIC
OCEAN

1   Amelonado
2   Beniano
3   Contamana
4   Criollo
5   Curaray
6   Guiana
7   Iquitos
8   Juruá
9   Marañón
10 Nacional
11 Nanay
12 Purús

Ghosts of the Maya Mountains

Belize, 1993–95

In 1993, while Volker Lehmann was getting to know the forests of Amazonia, a long-haired hippie named Jacob Marlin was two thousand miles to the north, hiking high into the pristine wilderness of Belize's Bladen Nature Reserve, the crown jewel of Central American preserves. The Bladen's soaring peaks and impenetrable jungle held the greatest diversity of plants and animals north of the Amazon, and its inaccessibility meant it was all virtually untouched. Jacob had just hired on as the herpetologist on a privately funded expedition to assess its diversity. It was only the second scientific foray into the area ever undertaken. For him, it was the kind of gig he'd always dreamed about.

Jacob had grown up in the urban jungle of Washington, D.C., in the 1980s, but he fell in love with the natural world, especially reptiles, and lit out for the wild while still a teenager. "I didn't really want to stay in the States," he told me in 2022 when I visited his environmental education center in the Belize rainforest, the Belize Foundation for Research and Environmental Education (BFREE). "I didn't want to do the nine-to-five. I wanted to go see tropical forests and I wanted to go catch snakes and crocodiles."

And he did! After knocking around the tropics for a few years, he wound up in Belize in the late 1980s, and fell hard. A New Jersey–sized hodgepodge of beaches, reefs, banana farms, and mountains, it had a whopping 160,000 people and very little going on.

"There were two paved roads," Jacob recalled with nostalgia. "There was one traffic light, and it was broken. I mean, there was nothing down here, man! If you couldn't build and fix everything you owned, no one was going to do it for you. And I loved that."

What Belize *did* have was the most conservation-minded government in the Americas. More than 70 percent of the country was still forested, and with few great options on the table, the government had decided to bank on ecotourism. Almost half the land was already protected in parks and reserves, and more were coming. For a young nature lover like Jacob, it was paradise.

And the Bladen Nature Reserve was its most paradisiacal place, one hundred thousand acres in the Maya Mountains, where no one was allowed to go without a research permit. Jacob's fifteen-member expedition had the place to themselves. They just had to get there. "We had to hike up the Bladen River for four days just to make base camp," Jacob explained. "On the way up, I remember passing wild cacao trees. But I had no idea what they were."

Their guide was an old Maya jaguar hunter named Arturo. "He was just an ox of a man," said Jacob. "Didn't really have any teeth, kind of hard to understand, but he was a wonderful guy. He took great care of us." Arturo showed them wild coffee, wild bananas, wild tomatoes, wild spinach. "There were wild things everywhere. I mean, we were eating off the forest, man."

These plants weren't the same as their domestic counterparts; they just made good substitutes. Jacob assumed the cacao was the same, and he gave it no more thought. He had his hands full. "We went to places no human had been since the days of the ancient Maya—not one, *countless* places! We came upon clay statues of monkey gods and jaguar gods. We saw burial grounds. Clearly no one had been there."

At least, not since the Maya civilization had collapsed a thousand years earlier. For the next two weeks, Jacob found himself exploring a world straight out of a fantasy novel. "All of a sudden, you'd be like, 'Oh my god, I think I see a cave opening!' And then you go in, and you walk for nine hours, and then you look down a hundred and fifty feet below you and you see a huge river flowing. And then you look to the side and there's Maya pottery and skeletons scattered everywhere. Then you *swim* out of the cave and you find these massive trees with, you know, two hundred and fifty spider monkeys swinging in them, and then there's a jaguar over there! That's what our fifteen-day expedition was like. When I came out, I was completely blown away."

In all the tropics, it was his favorite place he'd ever been, the most unspoiled. But there was no guarantee it was going to stay that way. The cash-strapped Belizean government had zero resources to devote to the Bladen—no rangers, no infrastructure for incoming researchers, no management plan. It was a park on paper only.

Jacob decided to see if he could change that. He put the word out that he was looking for property near the Bladen, and about a year later, Arturo told him about a 1,153-acre parcel for sale.

It couldn't have been more perfect. It was owned by a developer who had planned to put in a banana farm and never got around to it. It was beautiful forest, right on the edge of the Bladen, crawling with jaguars and ocelots and tapirs and howler monkeys and, more to Jacob's liking, boa constrictors and coral snakes and fer-de-lance, one of the world's deadliest vipers. There were dozens of different hummingbirds, scarlet macaws, and too many parrots to count.

And best of all, it fell at the intersection of four major reserves—the Bladen Nature Reserve, the Maya Mountain Forest Reserve, the Coxcomb Basin Wildlife Sanctuary, and the Deep River Forest Reserve—connecting them in unbroken jungle. Its loss would be devastating—and it was the perfect entry point into the Bladen.

Jacob cobbled together enough money to buy the land. Back in the States, he and his girlfriend threw all their belongings into a 1971 Land Cruiser and drove down to Belize for good. They lived in a tent on the property, exploring it bit by bit, making plans. They raised three kids in the jungle.

Jacob established BFREE. He met with the government and convinced it that the Bladen needed some tender loving care. Go for it, said the ministers. Just don't ask us for money.

No problem. Jacob made the rounds of international nongovernmental organizations (NGOs) and foundations, raising money. The government made him the first manager of the Bladen Nature Reserve. He created a management plan for the Bladen, built some huts, hired rangers. And then researchers started showing up to do their Ph.D.s in the reserve, and he built better housing. Then a real ranger station. Then a center for visiting student groups. And gradually, BFREE became a model of tropical conservation.

Meanwhile, he kept exploring the forest, and everywhere he went, Jacob noticed cacao trees. "It would be just one tree, growing in the middle of tall forest. And then ten meters later, another. And then hundreds of meters later, another. They didn't look planted. They were completely scattered." They were hard to spot in the understory, unless they had pods, in which case you couldn't miss them. The pods were bright red and purple and yellow, like Japanese lanterns advertising some secret speakeasy.

Wild cacao? Jacob noted it as a curiosity . . . and promptly put it out of his mind. "I was like, 'Cacao? Who cares?' I was focused on conservation and protected areas, and I was really expanding in that direction." Cacao sounded like agriculture, and Jacob wasn't into agriculture. He was a nature guy. If anything, agriculture was the enemy, the world's top driver of deforestation. "Cacao to me was not interesting. It was cool, yeah, but there's so many cool things here. So I didn't really think about it."

But that was going to change. Years later, Big Ag was going to find him. And he was going to have to deal with it, if BFREE was going to survive. And those strange, straggly cacao trees lurking in the understory were going to become his ace in the hole. Had he known more about cacao, he might have recognized signs of their specialness, but even then, he couldn't have guessed the truth. These trees scattered through the Maya Mountains were the most sought-after cacao variety in the world, and most chocolate makers had given up hope of ever finding them.

5

Rainforest Delight

Beni and La Paz, Bolivia, 1997–2000

As a general rule, the Amazon is not subtle. The greens are too green. The bugs are too buggy. The rivers too thick. The humid air laps at you like a mouth-breathing beast.

But even amid a sea of extremes, the Huanchaca Plateau rises into the realm of fantasy. The sheer cliffs of this ninety-three-mile-long mesa soar more than a thousand feet above the surrounding jungle, isolating a cloud-top world the size of a New England state. The explorer Percy Fawcett, who spent many years searching the Amazon for the Lost City of Z before disappearing into its maw in 1925, was the first European to size up Huanchaca, and his excited reports of the place, and the unique creatures that might have slipped notice on the plateau, were the inspiration for Arthur Conan Doyle's 1912 novel *The Lost World*.

So far, no dinosaurs have been reported atop Huanchaca, but its extraordinary biodiversity—not to mention the epic water-falls cascading off its flanks—led the Bolivian government to

designate it as a national park in the 1970s. Its foremost advocate was Noel Kempff Mercado, Bolivia's most famous biolo-
gist, who'd spent years documenting the park's life-forms.

But a high table along the Brazil-Bolivia border is also the
dreamiest of smuggler stopovers, and in 1986, Kempff Mercado
and his team were gunned down on the plateau when they landed
their plane on a makeshift landing strip and stumbled into a
massive cocaine-refining operation. Two years later, the park was
renamed Noel Kempff Mercado National Park.

In the 1990s, the park became the centerpiece of the largest
carbon-credits scheme ever attempted. The plan was the brain-
child of the Nature Conservancy, which convinced the Bolivian
government to stop all logging in the park and to make up for
the lost income by selling millions of dollars in carbon offsets to
companies generating carbon pollution elsewhere in the world.

But ending logging in the park would also mean the loss of
many jobs, so part of the plan involved finding new sustainable
enterprises for the people who lived there. Volker Lehmann
hired on with an outfit called Canopy Botanicals, whose team
was trying to do just that. They had surveyed the park, consulted
the locals, evaluated the international markets. And they had
a plan.

Walk the rainforest near the Bolivia-Brazil border, peer up
through the canopy, and you will see giants towering overhead.
Rising more than one hundred feet into the sky, these powerful
trees, some more than five centuries old, produce a crop of coco-
nuts the size of bocce balls clustered near the top. Do not let
one of these five-pound cannonballs drop on your head. *Do* find
the ones already on the ground and break them open. Inside, you

will discover a dozen or so wedge-shaped nuts, packed like orange slices.

These are Brazil nuts. Most people know Brazil nuts as the gargantuan standouts in cans of mixed nuts. Unfortunately, the stale nuts in those cans do nothing to highlight the amazing qualities of *Bertholletia excelsa*. When harvested fresh, they are one of the great treats of the rainforest.

And the trees can be found only there, along the borders between Bolivia, Brazil, and Peru. They can't be cultivated. For pollination, they depend on wild orchid bees, and the bees in turn depend on orchids for their mating ritual, which involves the males smearing themselves in juice from the orchid flowers to get the attention of the ladies. A male bee without his Eau d'Orchidée will get nowhere. So the bees need the orchids, which grow only in pristine rainforest, and the trees need the bees, as well as an extremely wet tropical climate. And that means they are limited to the last healthy stands of Amazonia.

As the poster child of sustainable agroforestry, Brazil nuts should sell for big money. But they don't. Few consumers know their story, and the nuts rarely reach international markets in good shape, so it's no surprise that most people think of them as little more than giant peanuts. The nuts do get harvested by locals and sold to suppliers, but prices are distressingly low.

Sadly, the trees are more valuable for their excellent wood. In Brazil, most of them have already been cut down, ironically leaving the future of Brazil nuts in Bolivia's hands. One of the best places to still find them is Noel Kempff Mercado National Park.

To the Canopy Botanicals team, Brazil nuts seemed like the perfect lever for park preservation. True, the plain nuts didn't sell for much as just another commodity, but turn them into a fancy treat, put them in front of American consumers with the conservation story front and center, and you might have a winner on your hands.

How to do that? Well, chocolate, of course. The optics couldn't be better. Wild Brazil nuts enrobed in wild Bolivian chocolate, all sustainably harvested in the Amazon. Hello, Whole Foods! The team already had a name: Rainforest Delight.

Volker was skeptical. He'd tasted wild Bolivian chocolate. There was no way you could coat precious Brazil nuts in the stuff and pass it off as a gourmet treat.

But then he tried a sample from an early test batch. And then he tried another, just to make sure the first one hadn't been a fluke. Volker Lehmann has a superb palate, honed on Europe's finest wines, cheeses, and chocolates. He could tell this was the real deal. Rich, creamy, nothing nasty about it. This couldn't possibly be made with wild cacao!

But it was. Made for Canopy Botanicals by a tiny factory in La Paz.

Volker couldn't believe it. How could this be so much better?

Well, that was just it. Most of the batches the factory had produced weren't this good. Not even close. But every now and then, a good batch of cacao came through, and it changed everything. They had no idea why some was better, but they needed a lot more of the good stuff. And that mystery was exactly what they were hoping Volker could solve. To start, he was going to have to meet their chocolate maker.

Downtown La Paz is a cobblestoned kaleidoscope of steep streets and tiny shops festooned with the colorful wares of what seems to be one endless street market. Aymara women in bowler hats hawk alpaca sweaters and magic charms and trash bags full of coca leaves. In the midst of this madness, Volker Lehmann stepped into a tiny candy shop called Bombonería Clavel. It was straight out of the 1940s, all wood and mirrors, everything sold by weight. The proprietor was a no-nonsense sixty-seven-year-old Jewish man named Irachmil Nudelman. He made all his own chocolate in his miniature factory, Gallo Mundial. And he was making Rainforest Delight.

Nudelman had been born in Poland. He and his family escaped the Nazis in 1939 and spent years on the move through Siberia, Uzbekistan, and Israel before finally landing in La Paz in 1955, where he taught himself to make chocolate, started a business, and raised a family.

Nudelman was the only chocolate maker in Bolivia working in the European tradition, and part of that tradition involved knowing how to get the off flavors out of cacao, because most of the cacao on the market was off. That was partly because of the poor natural flavor of most bulk beans, but also because of the postharvest practices of the farmers. More on that soon. For now, what matters is that European chocolate makers had long ago figured out that the secret to better-tasting cacao was to beat the hell out of it in a trough fitted with rollers and paddles, known as a "conche" (because the original was shell-shaped). As the solids, cocoa butter, and sugar are kneaded together for hours—or even days in the case of high-end chocolate—the nasty, volatile compounds are freed to escape into the air, or transformed into better-tasting molecules. Conching isn't perfect—you lose interesting aromas along with the unwanted ones—but it reliably produces smooth and inoffensive chocolate that flows seamlessly into the stream of commerce.

Irachmil Nudelman was the only chocolate maker in Bolivia conching his beans, and it showed. But he still had problems. Nudelman bought his beans from a wholesaler in La Paz, and he never knew what he was going to get. Every now and then, they were great, like the ones Volker had tried. Mostly, they were terrible, and no amount of conching could save them.

Everyone agreed that inconsistency would doom Rainforest Delight. They needed a steady supply of good beans. And they had no idea how to get them. Canopy Botanicals needed a cacao detective. Someone who could trace the beans to the source, figure out why some were good and some were not, and find a lot more of the good stuff.

Well, that was Volker's kind of gig. He knew agroforestry. He knew supply networks. He'd been curious about that cacao for years. And most important, he knew how to get around the Beni without getting killed.

The trail led to Santa Cruz, then to Trinidad, the small city that is the capital of the Beni. Well, calling it a "city" was a stretch. It was a two-story sprawl of concrete-block markets and motor-cycle repair shops, with macaws living in hollowed-out palm trunks downtown. Families spent the evening circling the central plaza on 150 cc motorbikes—kids, grandma, everyone perched on a single bike like circus performers. Even the taxis were motorbikes. But the bikes had nowhere to go. There was nothing beyond Trinidad but roadless wetlands.

If the Beni was the Wild West, Trinidad was the trading post. It was situated on the lower Mamoré River, just after it had snaked through a hundred miles of jungle. Traders went up the

Mamoré in their canoes, laden with rice and machetes and gasoline, and came out weeks later with cacao, hides, feathers, herbs, and wood.

Whenever Volker found cacao in one of the markets, he sampled it. And it was all foul. Some was bitter and sour. Some tasted like smoky ham, others like blue cheese and stinky feet. The worst offenders tipped toward manure.

Disappointing? Not at all! To Volker, it smelled like opportunity. By then, he'd read every technical book he could find on the production of chocolate, and the same word kept jumping out at him: "fermentation." Great chocolate requires beans that have been carefully fermented after harvest. As with wine, that's where all the dazzling flavor compounds get made. Skip that step, and your chocolate will be about as flavorful as burnt toast.

The key was the alcohol and vinegar produced as the sugary pulp fermented. As it saturated the beans, it dissolved the cells inside, breaking apart their bitter and astringent compounds and creating chemical chain reactions that resulted in a whole new suite of aromatic molecules, which, when roasted, bloomed into the full spectrum of chocolate flavor: nutty, toasty, buttery, winey, earthy, spicy, fruity, tart, and floral all at once.

But a whole lot of things had to go right for that to happen. The pods had to be picked at the peak of ripeness, and the fermentation had to be hot and fast enough to keep other stinky microbes from gaining a foothold. The beans had to soak in the vinegar long enough for the chemical reactions to start, but not so long that they tasted like salad dressing. And once the fermentation was complete, they had to be dried fast enough that no molds could form on the outside, but not so fast that the outer shells would harden before the interior moisture could escape, trapping rot inside. When it goes wrong, you end up with beans that taste sour, bitter, moldy, or a dozen different versions of gross.

Fermentation is both an art and a science, and its true masters are few and far between. It works best in a well-designed facility where conditions can be precisely controlled, but that's a rarity. The reality is that most cacao in the world is produced by poor farmers who have neither the time nor the expertise nor the infrastructure to do it that way, and who wouldn't be rewarded with higher prices even if they did. Instead, their goal is just to get the cacao dried and sold. No matter what it tastes like, someone will buy it. As they say in the industry, there's no cemetery for cocoa beans.

The kinds of gross Volker was getting in these Bolivian beans seemed a lot like the result of bad fermentation, and that excited him. At heart, Volker is a tinkerer. When he sees a system misfiring, just screaming out for a little good old German engineering, he can't resist the urge to tweak it until it's purring like a Mercedes. And the more he poked around wild cacao, the more he suspected that fermentation was where his wrench needed to go.

The big source of cacao, he learned, was a village called Baures, one hundred miles to the northeast. At least, it was one hundred miles as the toucan flies. But there were no roads to Baures, so the cacao arrived by a circuitous river route at least three times that long. Sometimes it arrived on horseback.

The stories people told him made no sense. They claimed there were whole forests of cacao in Baures, thousands of acres. He chalked that up to hyperbole—the tree he'd seen with the old Chimané woman had been solo, which seemed more natural—but still, he had to go find out.

No roads? No problem! Like every town in the coke-soaked Beni, Baures had an airstrip. So he chartered a bush plane and made the flight.

Below, a surprising landscape scrolled by. There were patches of dark jungle, but they were surrounded by a light-green sea of marshes and grasslands, broken by strangely rectangular lakes and strafed by flocks of white egrets. The whole landscape was etched in lines he couldn't make sense of: skinny ridges running straight as an arrow between the islands of forest. Other places, he could make out geometric patterns buried beneath the surface. He felt like he was gazing at giant runes, a secret message to be deciphered. It was beautiful, hypnotic, inscrutable. He could never have imagined it was about to become his new home.

6

Tranquility

Beni, Bolivia, 2001–03

B aures was a traditional Amazonian town, a grid of stucco buildings around a grassy central square. It was the home of the Baure people, an Indigenous group who had lived in small settlements scattered through the area until Jesuit missionaries arrived in the 1700s and centralized everyone. Volker scored a meeting with the mayor, who was both pleased and surprised by this outside interest in the cacao.

Yes, the mayor confirmed, there were forest islands of cacao in the wetlands around Baures. Thirty-six in all, hundreds of thousands of trees. They called them chocolatales, and they had always been there.

During the wet season, when the cacao was ripe, families would spend days traveling to the chocolatales by canoe. They'd camp in the forest for weeks, picking the pods, opening them, and drying the beans on mats in the sun. They'd keep a little for their own use, but mostly it was a cash crop. They would borrow money from traders to buy food for the trip, then pay them back in beans, and sell anything extra. It was one of the only ways to make a little cash in such a remote place.

That tradition actually dated back to the Jesuits, who arrived in the region in the late 1600s and seized on the wild cacao trees growing in the area as a way to finance their missions. Cacao production became one of the main industries of the mission towns in the 1700s, with the Baure people given little choice in the matter. They did the work, and the Jesuits shipped the cacao to Spain, where it became famous. Madrid gourmets considered Beniano cacao, with its intense fragrance and low bitterness, to be the finest in the world, even better than the Criollo from Mexico.

In the late 1700s, Europe's monarchs eliminated the Jesuits, who had grown too powerful and threatened their rule, and the outside world forgot all about Beniano cacao. But the Baure people continued the practice, selling to local buyers for the domestic market.

Now that practice was dying. As people in Bolivia's cities switched to powdered cocoa mix, demand for the traditional drinking patties was falling. The prices for wild cacao dropped too low to justify the work. People were giving up on the yearly harvest trips. A few chocolatales had even been cleared for cattle grazing.

Volker couldn't believe what he was hearing. He'd stumbled into the Shangri-la of cacao. While the NGOs were spending millions to try to invent a sustainable forest economy, one had been in place for centuries, right under their noses. And now it was endangered.

The next step was easy. He had to see these chocolatales for himself. But they were miles out of town, and it was the dry season. Canoeing was not an option. So he hired a horse and a guide, and he hit the range.

Volker had done a little riding in his youth, but that didn't prepare him for the torture of the tropical pampas. Six hours in the saddle, the sun beating down. First he couldn't feel his legs. Then he couldn't feel anything. Horseflies opened bloody wounds on him and his horse. He began to see mirages on the shimmering horizon. First water, then beasts.

Finally, one of the dark shapes in the distance stopped shimmering. As they drew closer, it solidified into what looked like an island floating over the wetlands. It was a chocolatal raised just a few feet above the wetland, high and dry enough that trees could survive the three months of annual flooding.

They tied up their horses, took out their machetes, and slipped into the forest, following footpaths worn by generations of feet. Ceiba trees and palms towered above them, but the understory was full of small trees with clustered trunks and broad, waxy leaves. It was all cacao. Thousands of trees, all connected by footpaths.

His guide showed him how the harvesting was done, and Volker resisted the urge to do cartwheels. As he'd suspected, decent fermentation and drying were impossible in such a remote and primitive environment. The pickers would just open the pods and spread the beans on the ground, or on cloths if they had them. Quality control was nonexistent. Rot was unavoidable. Room for improvement . . . massive.

Volker returned from Baures and gave his partners a glowing report. Yes, he'd figured out the quality problem, and yes, it looked fixable. Fire up the chocolate mill.

And then a band of terrorists flew two Boeing 767s into the World Trade Center and everything fell apart. The cost of air transport soared, the world economy sputtered, businesses pulled back from unnecessary ventures like the Noel Kempff Mercado park project, and Canopy Botanicals pulled the plug on Rainforest Delight.

After he got over the shock, he considered his options. His whole life, he'd been convinced the world was going to hell. His parents had lost everything in World War II and struggled terribly through the German recession that followed. Volker had lived through the oil crisis of the 1970s, the nuclear threats of the '80s, and too many economic shocks to count. Now this. Maybe the world really was going to hell. Maybe he'd just stay in Baures for a while.

Volker continued exploring the region by foot, boat, and horseback. He fell in love with the endless wetlands and hundred-mile views. Friendly people. More wildlife than he'd ever seen: howler monkeys, capybaras, crocodiles, jaguars. Tons of cacao in desperate need of a market. The classic challenges of frontier life, but none of the modern insanities.

And then came the moment that whipped the trajectory of his life in a new and unexpected direction. To his astonishment, he learned that one of the thirty-six chocolatales was for sale. He was surprised how the news gripped him.

"Show it to me," he said.

All the cacao forests that fell within the boundaries of Baures itself were owned communally by the Baures people, but the handful that fell outside Baures were on private land. The one for sale was part of a collection of estates owned by a wealthy ranching family with territory all over the Beni. The thirteen-thousand-acre parcel had been inherited by one of the family's children who lived overseas. She was looking to unload it.

It was about five hundred acres of forest and another eight hundred of wetland. No buildings of any kind. Pristine jungle. It even had a name, bestowed by some long-gone owner on both the land and the sparkling arroyo that ran along its edge: Tranquilidad—*Tranquility*.

Volker walked the forest, astonished at the number of cacao trees. It was shady, warm, and still. The ground was smooth with waxy leaves. The whole forest was surrounded by a ring ditch a mile long and ten feet deep, cacao trees sprouting from it. He tucked it away in the back of his mind as another mystery to investigate.

The cacao trees had a naturally harmonious spacing between them, like the columns of some ancient temple. He walked from tree to tree, admiring the tiny, jewel-like white flowers blooming straight from the trunks. He opened a pod and tasted the juice. Capuchin monkeys scolded him from the canopy. The ground was nice and high, unlikely to flood.

Volker knew that if he didn't buy it, the next buyer would probably clear the forest. He felt something tug at him. If the world really was going to hell, it might be a good idea to have a piece of land where you could go when it did. But there was more to it than that. After a lifetime of teaching other people to grow food, he was yearning to do it himself.

The asking price was thirteen thousand dollars. He had ten thousand dollars to his name. He offered it all. "If it suits you," he said, "take it."

They took it. And suddenly he had his own cacao forest. And something to prove.

He built himself a tiny house out of wood and brick, with a thatched palm roof. Then he added an even tinier shed where he could ferment and dry his beans.

And that's when things got a little bit cosmic. As he cleared the spot, out of the red earth came a broken clay pot. And then another. And another.

They were beautiful, with fluted necks and intricate etched patterns. As Volker kept digging, the treasures kept coming. Little axes, with notches for strings so they could be hung up. A doll for a kid to play with.

He stared at the objects for a while. Then he walked out into the forest and stared at that ring ditch some more. Then he made some calls.

Eventually, he got in touch with an archaeologist named Clark Erickson who had been working in the Beni for years. Erickson visited Tranquilidad, walked the site, and said yep, this was the exact pattern he was finding all over the Beni. Ring ditches surrounding high ground filled with cacao trees, centuries-old artifacts buried underneath. Of the 20,900 hectares of land Erickson counted inside the ring ditches, 5,700 of it was cacao forest.

Or orchard, more to the point.

All the chocolatales were growing on ancient settlements that had been established on the patches of high ground. The ditches were for defense. Each would have been backed by a high wooden fence, with a collection of houses inside. And they were part of a massive network of terraces, pyramids, causeways, and canals that stretched across thousands of square miles. That explained the lines Volker had seen from the air. The people had lived and farmed on the islands, safe from flooding, and traveled between them on raised causeways, or canoed in canals that ran beside the causeways. And they cultivated cacao on the high ground.

So this part of the Amazon was not a primordial wilderness. It was the overgrown orchards and plazas and streets of a sophisticated culture, now known as the Casarabe. A thousand years ago, several million people lived in this part of Bolivia and Brazil, the largest community of native people in the Amazon. It may have been the source of rumors about the Lost City of Z.

And these trees were its descendants. One of the extraordinary qualities of the cacao tree is that it never really dies. The trees sprout multiple trunks, and the trunks eventually fall over and resprout, continuing the endless cycle of decay and rebirth that marks life in the tropics. So Tranquilidad was, in a sense, a ghost island of ancient beings. As Volker settled into life there, he began to see himself as just a small part of a larger story the place was telling.

And it was a story that needed to be told to the wider world. Volker was well aware of the surge of interest in quality chocolate under way in Europe, especially cacao from exotic origins. If he could figure out a way to fix the fermentation, and the cacao was as good as he hoped, it might garner international interest. Then the beans would command more money, the pickers could survive, the tradition would endure, and the chocolatales might be preserved against the encroaching ranches. Clearly, it was now or never.

He set up the artifacts on a little altar in the corner of his house, to remind himself. And then he got to work. He had some chocolate to make. The place was counting on him.

Volker's vision for his new enterprise went something like this: Get the Valrhonas of the world excited about his wild cacao. Ship them the beans. They make the chocolate and tell the story. They pay him a premium, he pays the harvesters a premium, the chocolatales gain recognition, everybody wins.

But for any of that to happen, he needed to let the world of chocolate know about the beans. So he boned up on fermentation, teaching himself through trial and error, shuttling back and forth between Tranquilidad during the harvest season and his family in Santa Cruz during the offseason. He kept changing the parameters of each batch, playing with time and temperature and drainage, until he hit on a formula that showed the beautiful fragrance of the beans. He began to wonder if the Jesuits had been on to something. Maybe there was a reason the Madrileños of the 1700s went crazy for Beni chocolate. Maybe there was some special mojo here.

When he felt confident in his abilities, he harvested a few kilos and fermented and dried them to his best persnickety German standards. He made the rounds of international trade shows, beans in hand, excited to blow some minds. He couldn't wait to see the expert buyers nibble the beans, hear his story, and fall all over themselves to get involved.

So he showed up in his one suit, and . . . nobody cared. As soon as they glanced at his name tag and saw "Bolivia," they kept on moving. These guys were pros, they'd been in the business for years, and Bolivia was not on their bingo card.

Even when someone did take a look at the beans, it didn't help. The wild Beni beans were just half the size of normal beans. They simply looked wrong to anyone in the industry, and they wouldn't work on standard equipment.

"I was running around with these small beans for two years!" Volker told me. "Nobody wanted them. I sent them to Scharffen Berger. I sent them to Japan. No good, no good, no good. I started investing more effort, time, money, everything, with no promise that it would work out. I was just convinced that the cacao was wonderful."

But he couldn't convince anyone in the biz that the cacao was wonderful. Eventually, Volker blew through his cash reserves with nothing to show for it. Broke, depressed, discouraged, he began wondering what else he could do to survive.

And then, finally, somebody got curious. It was a man named Stefan Bloch who worked for a Swiss company called Pronatec that specialized in importing sustainable foods from the developing world. Bloch had no preconceived notions of where good cacao should come from or what it should look like. And Volker's story was right up his alley.

To Volker's shock, Bloch asked if he could visit Tranquilidad to check out the situation. Volker rolled out the royal carpet for the guy, walked him into the forest, showed him the trees. They cracked open a pod and tasted the pulp. Volker could tell he was falling under the spell. They walked and talked until they came to an arroyo and surprised a huge black caiman that thrashed its way into the shallows. After their hearts stopped racing, they decided it was a sign and named the project Crocodile Cacao.

Pronatec had strong relationships with food producers in Switzerland, including Felchlin, the century-old chocolate maker that had launched its own Grand Cru line in 1999 to compete with Bonnat and Valrhona. Felchlin was playing catch-up, scrambling to lock down some good sources of beans, looking for ways to set itself apart. On Bloch's recommendation, it agreed to take a look at Volker's weird beans. Could he send a few kilos for lab tests?

Volker sent off the beans right away. After so much frustration, he tried not to get his hopes up. What if the beans weren't as special as he thought? What if nobody cared?

A few weeks later, Felchlin reached out. The lab experiments were . . . intriguing. But the tiny size was problematic. Could he please send four hundred kilos of dried beans to Switzerland so they could run some tests on the big equipment.

Oh yes, he said. Absolutely! No problem!

Then he walked outside and stared into his chocolatal and wondered how the hell he was going to do that.

He spent two sweaty months in the jungle picking by hand. He worked dawn to dusk until he'd personally harvested a ton of fresh cacao. He fermented and dried it as best he could and sent it to Switzerland.

Then he crossed his fingers. And waited. And waited some more.

Finally, the call came. The beans were so small that when the first two hundred kilos went through the winnowing machine, which is supposed to just blow off the papery outer shells, it blew all two hundred kilos straight down the waste chute.

Volker said he was very, very sorry to hear that.

BUT. They'd fidgeted with the equipment . . . And the next two hundred kilos . . . well, could he please come to Switzerland for a meeting?

So he cleaned himself up, dusted off his suit, and crossed the Atlantic. At Felchlin's corporate headquarters in Schwyz, he was ushered into a conference room. Volker laughed when he recalled the meeting. "There were all these serious faces sitting around a table. It was very Swiss." On the table were five chocolate samples.

"They said, 'One of these is made with your cacao. See if you can pick it out.'"

In the silent room, all eyes on him, he slowly tasted each sample, rolling the chocolate on his tongue and letting it melt so the aromatics would release. One of them was smooth and rich, with a deep nuttiness he knew well. He pointed to it and said, "That one."

"You're right," they said. "And we love it."

Felchlin was all in. They'd never tasted anything like this cacao, and they had big plans for it. They wanted to make a whole new bar, unlike any that had been made before. The world's first *wild* chocolate. They already had a name for it: Cru Sauvage.

And then came the big question: How many tons could he get them?

Volker laughed again when he recalled his answer. "I said, 'Well, ummm, errr . . . actually . . . I have no idea.'" He confessed that he'd never done this before. He didn't even know how to guess.

It was not the answer Felchlin wanted to hear, but the executives said, Okay, fine, we'll start small. Just get us as much as you can.

Volker walked out of the conference room in triumph. He'd seen something no one else had, and his vision was about to become reality. Sure, it would be small at first, but this thing could get big. Really big.

And he was right again. But he had no idea what he was in for. Over the next decade, Cru Sauvage would take him on a wild ride. It would make him famous. But it would also nearly destroy him.

7

In the Shadows

Belize and Guatemala, mid-2000s

In December 2006, Jacob Marlin was in a Cessna, soaring high above the Belize jungle. "It's a trip I do every year," he told me, "just me and a videographer, flying over this area to document any illegal logging or roadbuilding." That's an ongoing problem in Central America, and Jacob was trying to help out the eternally undermanned government. When he spotted illegal activity, he'd film it and report it to the authorities. But what he saw this time put his heart in his throat. "Damned if I don't see a yellow bulldozer, with a line of clay behind it, heading straight through the forest toward BFREE!"

It was even possible the bulldozer had already crossed the line onto BFREE land. Back then, BFREE was surrounded by unbroken forest in all directions, so there were no obvious demarcations. After they landed, Jacob hiked out to the area, intercepted the bulldozer, and put an end to the incursion, which turned out to be part of a scheme to sell off government land for banana and pineapple farms.

Though Jacob had stopped the assault before it reached BFREE, the experience rattled him. He'd always been focused entirely on conserving wildlands. To him, that was the only habitat that really mattered. Agriculture was just another form of development, not to mention the biggest driver of deforestation in the world. But the Belize government was banking hard on agriculture for its economic future and for food security, and Jacob realized he was going to have to make his peace with it. "I was like, 'Goddammit, this is a real issue, and it's going to become a much bigger issue.'" He needed to find less damaging forms of agriculture that could double as habitat and could serve as buffers around core reserves.

And that's when he thought of the cacao in his forests. "We started finding more and more of these trees. And they didn't all look the same. Some of the pods were yellow when ripe. Some were orange. Some were orange-purple. Some were green when ripe, some multicolored. They had different shapes and sizes. And what I noticed was that sometimes a tree would be in eighty percent shade in the middle of a forest, or ninety percent shade, and it was covered in pods!"

Jacob couldn't think of another fruit that could produce in that kind of environment. Certainly not the hybrid cacao grown in full sunshine on plantations around the world, which had long ago had its shade tolerance bred out of it. "Cacao is horrible!" he conceded. "Look at Africa! It's destroying national parks. It's eradicating species."

But maybe not this cacao . . . Suddenly, he got cacao-curious. "We decided, well, shit, man, let's make some chocolate! Just as a hobby. If nothing else, we could eat chocolate here."

Although Jacob didn't realize it at the time, he was part of a home-chocolate-making revolution that was just getting started. Traditionally, chocolate had been considered too complicated and capital-intensive to do at the hobby level. You needed big, expensive equipment and lots of professional knowledge. In the twentieth century, a handful of giant corporations like Cargill and Barry Callebaut and Blommer made most of the world's chocolate and supplied it to all the small chocolate companies and chocolatiers.

But an Oregon man named John Nanci changed all that when he launched his website, Chocolate Alchemy, in 2004. Nanci was both a home brewer and a home coffee roaster, and he was aware how both those areas had also once been considered out-of-bounds for amateurs, until better access to information and entry-level equipment had led to an explosion in hobbyists, and then an explosion in craft production as many of those hobbyists decided to take their passions professional. Nanci hoped to do the same for chocolate. And he did. Chocolate Alchemy became the go-to site for small-scale equipment, cacao beans, and how-to instructions, and it launched a new generation of American bean-to-bar chocolate makers, both amateur and professional.

Jacob bought a little tabletop chocolate-making kit and taught himself to ferment and dry his beans. "We ended up finding about three hundred of these wild trees on the property. So every year, we'd go out there with backpacks and sticks and harvest the pods. And I'd bring it all up to the station and make chocolate."

And it came out better than he ever imagined. "People would come through here and be like, 'God, that stuff's really special!'" Those in the know even pointed out that the white color of the beans was unusual, and important. So Jacob did his research. "The more I learned, the more I was like, 'Maybe we got something.' You know, the color of the beans, that means they're probably a Criollo variety. And I didn't know much about what that meant, but I knew it was a relic cacao, not grown much, basically gone."

But it seemed to Jacob that if there was any place such a relic could have survived the ages, unnoticed, it was right there. "The Maya Mountains are older than any other piece of landscape in Central America, and the heart of it all is the Bladen Nature Reserve. It's the least explored, least disturbed, most unspoiled place. Every time we do an expedition up there, we make some crazy new discovery. A new salamander, a snail, a harpy eagle, a tree." As he told me this, Jacob paused and cast his eyes into the jungle, grasping for words to capture something you clearly had to be deep in the Bladen to understand. "I don't know. There's a *feeling* you get up there. It just feels like this stuff has always been here. It just feels *old*."

Across the border in Guatemala, the future manager of Jacob Marlin's cacao reforesting project was staring at the bare fields of his family farm and wondering what to do. Erick Ac was a Maya man in his thirties with several small children and a farm in the Guatemalan highlands near Cobán that he shared with his six brothers. They called it Finca Ana Maria, after their mother.

The farm was mostly traditional cornfields, but Erick had some new ideas. He'd been working as an agronomist with the International Union for the Conservation of Nature, teaching Indigenous communities in the vicinity of Lachuá Lake National Park to convert to organic agriculture, and he wanted to make similar changes on his own farm.

"Corn is very intensive," he told me when I met him in Guatemala in 2023. "You have to remove the whole forest. You don't leave anything on the land." Cornfields had to be cleared or burned to bare earth, and maintained with aggressive applications of chemicals. Erick wanted to grow something that could restore the health of the land. He did his research, and one crop jumped out at him: cacao. "It's a really good crop," he said. "A lot of co-benefits." From what he'd learned, shade-grown cacao could be grown organically, would conserve soil and water, would sequester carbon, and could even serve as pretty good habitat for wildlife.

But he also knew that the standard cacao grown in Guatemala would be economically ruinous. Most cacao in Guatemala gets sold dirt cheap to Mexico, the big market for drinking chocolate. But at those prices, a small farm like Finca Ana Maria could never produce enough to make the numbers work.

Erick thought there was another way. In his years of consulting around Guatemala, he'd encountered a few farms with European connections that were growing specialty cacao and selling it directly to European importers for a lot more money. What these importers were looking for in particular was Criollo, which in Guatemala meant any of the old white-beaned varieties that had grown there since ancient times. Although most farmers in Guatemala had switched to the modern, disease-resistant dark-beaned varieties pushed by government agronomists and nurseries, there was still a lot of Criollo around the highlands on the older farms.

So Erick began collecting pods from every white-beaned cacao tree he came across and planting the seeds back at Finca Ana Maria. He also took cuttings from the trees and grafted clones in his own nursery. Soon he had an experimental garden of white-beaned Criollo variants that he could play around with, learning what they liked and what they didn't. At the time, Erick still believed the conventional wisdom that the old Criollos weren't nearly as productive as modern hybrids, especially when grown organically under shade. He just hoped the beans would command enough of a premium to make up the difference.

The results of his experiment would amaze him. Although it would take years of trial and error, he would learn that this was yet another example of conventional wisdom that had never been put to the test. It turned out the world had simply forgotten how to grow Criollo. When treated right, this ancient cacao produced yields that blew away what most cacao farmers were getting with their conventional hybrids. Combined with the huge premium Criollo was earning on the market, that led Erick to the same kind of conclusions Jacob was drawing across the border in Belize. Maybe cacao didn't have to be the scourge of the tropics it was made it out to be. Maybe it could be just the opposite.

8

The Beni Hustle

Beni, Bolivia, late 2000s

By 2005, the world of craft chocolate was primed for Cru Sauvage, and Felchlin was ready to roll it out at full commercial scale. That meant no more cutesy experiments with four hundred kilos. To launch a flagship product like Cru Sauvage, they needed enough to fill an entire shipping container—about fifteen tons.

That's typical for goods in the modern world. Everything gets shipped in steel containers, and the price to use a container (generally thousands of dollars) is the same whether it's full or half empty. The numbers work a whole lot better if you can fill it. But for a solo player like Volker, that was a huge hill of beans.

By then, Volker knew that Tranquilidad itself could produce only a few tons. The rest he was going to have to bring in from other chocolatales around Baures, fermenting and drying everything in his greenhouse. And that meant he needed a ton of cash. He'd have to expand his facilities, hire workers, and pay the pickers for all that cacao months in advance of when he'd finally get paid by Felchlin. A ton of cash! His best guess was fifty thousand dollars.

To Volker, it seemed logical for Felchlin to front him the dough. "But they weren't interested," he told me. "They didn't want to have skin in the game."

You can see it from Felchlin's point of view. They hadn't been around for a hundred years because they let romance cloud their business vision. They were happy to pay a good price for the beans. But they weren't about to get sucked into a speculative venture in the Amazon.

Fortunately, Pronatec, his original Crocodile Cacao partner, came to the rescue. "They gave me the money," said Volker, "just on my blue eyes. And they said, 'Okay, we hope you come back with cacao!'"

Yeah, umm, how to do that?

Well, for starters, he bought himself a dirt bike and rode hundreds of miles across the range, visiting any town in the Beni that might have cacao. It was a rough ride, but it was better than the horse. He set up buying posts in each town, hiring locals to be his agents and forking over big wads of cash. He told them to dry the beans on tarps, not the ground. They showed him their moth-eaten jaguar hides and cow skins. So he flew in a bunch of tarps from Santa Cruz and handed them out.

But that wouldn't solve the main conundrum: how to ferment beans in remote locations with no facilities. Volker experimented with different methods and came up with a winner: if you hung the cacao from the trees in coffee sacks after harvest, the pulp juice would drip out at just the right rate to ferment the beans without pickling them. He taught it to the skeptical pickers and explained that those were the only beans he'd be buying. He explained again about the premium he'd be paying. He kept in touch with everyone by shortwave radio.

And almost everyone came through. He wound up with eighteen tons of dried beans at his Trinidad warehouse. He loaded them onto a riverboat and sent them on a winding, two-thousand-mile journey toward La Paz. Volker flew to La Paz ahead of the boat and rented an old racquetball court to use as a warehouse. He didn't sleep for a week while he waited for the beans to arrive.

Finally, they showed up. He immediately opened the sacks . . . and his heart sank. About 10 percent had turned moldy on the river trip. So he hired eight people to help him, and they spent the next two weeks on the floor of the racquetball court, sorting all eighteen tons of tiny beans by hand.

When he had fifteen good tons, he packed them into a container and trucked it over the carnage known in Bolivia as the road system, up a fifteen-thousand-foot mountain pass and down to the sea, where a feeder vessel took it to Panama and loaded it onto a giant container ship, which carried it through the canal, across the Atlantic, and into port in Rotterdam, where yet another feeder vessel carried it up the Rhine to Switzerland.

Where Felchlin transformed it into Cru Sauvage.

Soon the pros were getting their hands on their first bars of Cru Sauvage and posting rave reviews. Many still refused to believe there was such a thing as wild cacao, especially in Bolivia, but whatever this stuff was, it was mind-blowing.

The chocolate blogger Mark Christian was especially impressed by how different it was from the other top bars of the time. "It's a time machine," he told me. "You're getting this taste of *way back when*, both wild *and* refined. To me, that's a provi-dential bar."

The retailer Matt Caputo initially doubted the flavor would measure up to the design. "You know, Felchlin's good, but I'd never been blown away by anything. I thought it was a really cool mold, super long, super thin, with this beautiful feather imprint along it, but I wasn't expecting much. But when I popped it into my mouth, I immediately recognized that it was vastly more interesting than anything else they'd made. It was like perfumed woods, pipe tobacco, all these earthy, nutty, caramelly, *beautiful* flavors. Just super sophisticated. Sometimes I talk about choco-late like music, and this was like a classic symphony orchestra."

The upshot: the bar was a hit, and Felchlin needed even more beans for next season. This time, two containers: thirty tons instead of fifteen.

And that terrified Volker. He'd pulled off a miracle the first time, but he didn't know if he could do it again.

On Volker Lehmann's list of life goals, "cacao kingpin" had never ranked highly. His sweet spot would have been to produce a few tons a year at Tranquilidad, to tightly control every aspect of the fermentation and drying, to be part of one of the world's great chocolates, and to let the accolades roll in. But the ultimate goal was to create an economic shot in the arm for the whole region, and that required scale.

So he agreed to make it happen. And that, he confessed to me when we were in Bolivia, huddling under a roof to wait out a downpour, was his great mistake. "I had no intention to dig into this jungle," he said, gazing balefully into the rain. "I wasn't coming here to buy a piece of land and start doing all this. I was just looking for some stupid cacao in the forest. They said, 'Get us cacao.' And I said, 'Okay, I'll see what I can do. I'll identify people, and they'll deliver. Mission complete.' Well, you see what happened."

Actually, I didn't. What happened? "I fell into the trap. Because when I saw the cacao, I said, 'Oh, this cacao is no good, badly fermented. What can I do to improve it?' And that was a mistake. Because then I got curious."

By 2007, Volker's empire was expanding at *Breaking Bad* speed. He was paying dozens of middlemen to be his buyers. Building fermentation houses in the bush. Chartering Cessnas so he could check on quality. Renting storage rooms in seedy towns and paying guards to watch them. Rolling every euro back into the business, and borrowing more besides.

Any of Bolivia's cocaine kingpins would have recognized the fundamentals of his business. And they'd have recognized the next development: competition. As word got out about wild Bolivian cacao, new players jumped into the game.

Some of the newbies were chocolate companies. Others were nonprofits interested in sustainable development. At first, this seemed like a win. But NGOs have a very different relationship to projects than for-profit enterprises, and they sometimes have a destabilizing effect on the laws of supply and demand. Their focus is not the market, but their funders.

"They just jump on the bandwagon," Volker lamented to me. "They make a deal with an Indigenous group, get some nice photos, then they run to their funders. They're always going for big numbers. How many thousands of hectares conserved? How many small farmers? How many jaguars saved? Then they ask, 'Where does Volker sell his stuff? We'll try there!' "

Suddenly, well-endowed parties with no experience in the chocolate business were competing to get their hands on any wild cacao they could find. "Things got totally out of hand," said Volker. "Prices skyrocketed." Cacao exploded from about forty cents a pound to more than two dollars, fermented or not. "They were overpaying for almost any type of cacao, no quality whatsoever. Just winning the spot by paying more."

In a way, this was indeed Mission Accomplished. Volker's dream of creating a new forest economy that preserved the environment while bringing money to the area was coming true. People's lives improved. Interest in the chocolatales returned. It was textbook sustainable development.

Except it was an artificial economy, and it wasn't sustainable for businesses like Volker's. By 2009, he found himself priced out of the market he'd created. "It was like I had this little snowball," he said. "And I rolled it and rolled it, and then it just went out of my hand and kept rolling."

He needed a new supply. Cacao that hadn't yet exploded in price.

And that was one advantage he still had over the competition. These newcomers had no experience in the region. They were just flying into Baures and buying any beans they could find. But he had twenty years of connections all over the Beni. And he worked his connections for any leads on new sources of wild cacao.

And eventually, he found one.

In Trinidad, Volker got to know a trader named Aurelio Rivera. Aurelio and his brother Angel had grown up on a remote homestead a few days upriver from Trinidad on the Mamoré River, one of the wildest remaining wildernesses in Bolivia. They knew everyone, and they made their living buying goods from the river families, piling everything precariously into canoes, and selling it down in Trinidad. Those goods included a little bit of cacao.

Volker liked Aurelio. He was smart, hardworking, and more ambitious than most people living out on the Mamoré. Aurelio explained that what he was bringing to Trinidad was just a drop in the bucket. He painted a picture of thousands of acres of cacao lining the Mamoré and its tributaries, most of it rotting in the jungle. There was little market for it, the prices were terrible, and it was too remote, so most people didn't bother with it.

All music to Volker's ears. If there was enough cacao, maybe he could set up a whole buying center upriver, with covered areas for fermentation and drying. He could bring the market to the people. And Aurelio could run it for him.

That sounded good to Aurelio, so he set up some meetings between Volker and the people who lived on the river. Volker would have to show up, make friends, prove he was for real, and convince them it was in their best interest.

Of course, the Mamoré was also the autobahn of cocaine smuggling, one of the most dangerous alleys of an extremely dangerous region. But he needed to make it happen. And he had confidence in his abilities in the bush. So he made plans for the expedition.

And that, of course, was when I got in touch with him. And if he ever thought, well, this is a pretty weird spot to bring a journalist . . . he never mentioned it to me.

9

Deep Water

Beni, Bolivia, 2010

For two gringos to drop out of the sky in the Beni generally means one of two things: they are DEA, or they are smugglers themselves, neither of which seemed like it was going to be a plus for our four gun-toting friends. But there was enough weirdness in the situation that I didn't know what to think. The pilot was just staring out of the cockpit at the men. He'd gone all white. Bad sign. Slowly, he opened his window and said that he had to leave right away because a storm was coming in.

For a moment, nobody said anything. Then the leader of the four men jerked his chin, and the pilot spun the plane around and vanished into the sky like a ghost. As the engine faded, the sounds of the birds and bugs filled the seconds. Mosquitoes settled on my face, but I didn't dare swat them.

Finally, Volker spoke. "So I suppose we owe you a landing fee," he said.

The leader of the men chewed on this for a moment, then slowly nodded. "Five thousand bolivianos," he suggested. About $750.

That struck me as high but doable, considering the circumstances, and I felt a moment of relief. But Volker shrugged and said, "Unfortunately, we are very poor."

The guy looked us up and down and cocked an eyebrow.

"No, realmente!" Volker continued. He explained that we were meeting with the Yurucaré to start a new cacao project, and the whole thing was on a shoestring budget. He talked and talked and talked, funneling twenty years of cacao hunting into a single monologue, until the guys were either convinced or bored silly.

At the end of his rambling, Volker said we could probably spare five hundred bolivianos. Seventy-five bucks. That dropped my stomach a notch or two, but the men glanced at one another, and the leader slowly nodded. The money changed hands, and we all stood around awkwardly for a few moments until a dugout canoe with two people aboard came around the river bend and pulled up to the riverbank near the cabin. It was Aurelio, Volker's partner for this venture and our ride to the Yurucaré village of El Combate, three hours downstream, where the big meeting would take place. He had a rifle, too, but he chatted with the cabin guards like they were old friends. Maybe they were. At the end of the conversation, the guards threw in a bonus copy of a beat-up John Grisham paperback some previous party had left in the cabin, gave us a glass of water, and wished us a good trip.

Volker and I piled our stuff into the middle of the canoe and covered it with a tarp. We climbed over the pile and settled into the only open spots on the boat, and at last we were set free on the river. It was a churning brown monster, hissing as its sediment-filled waters raked through the flooded vegetation. Thunderheads grumbled above. The waterline lapped perilously close below. I feared for my stuff, but I was eager to get rolling. If all went well, we'd reach Combate, strike a deal, and then continue down the Mamoré, buying cacao and rallying riverside communities to the cause, all the way to Trinidad, several days downriver. It seemed like a solid plan.

Dante was our pilot. I never got a last name. The name struck me as inauspicious, but honestly, after bidding goodbye to our narco friends, I was enthusiastic about everything. The blue and gold macaws flapping gently from bank to bank, always in pairs. The pink river dolphins surfacing near the boat and exhaling with soft gasps. The thunder. The drum roll of cicadas up and down the riverbank. And the big fat wad of coca leaves in my left cheek.

A few years earlier, Evo Morales, the leader of Bolivia's coca growers, had been elected Bolivia's first Indigenous president. He ended the DEA's eradication efforts and then, for good measure, expelled the U.S. ambassador. More than ever, the country was awash in the stuff, and Dante seemed to be consuming his fair share. He had an eternal quid in his maw, so I'd begged for a little from the pouch on his belt. I stuffed the dried leaves inside my cheek, added a smidge of baking soda to start the chemical reaction, and let the alkaloids ooze into my bloodstream.

First my tongue and cheek went numb, then things began to occur to me. One was that there is no better way to float down the Amazon than on the wings of a mild coca high. Another was that it was a crying shame that cocaine has messed everything up, because natural coca is a wonder. It simply makes whatever you happen to be doing the most deeply satisfying thing in the world. Three hours on a hard wooden seat? Half a day without food? No problem.

Aurelio was curled up in the bow of the boat with his rifle, scanning the banks for bushmeat. If Dante's vibe was car mechanic, all belly, ball cap, and grease-smeared shirt, Aurelio was more cowboy: lanky build, thin mustache, white gambler hat. At a bend in the river, he gestured. Dante steered us toward the edge. I peered into the understory at the surreal sight. The trees were standing in several feet of floodwater, grooved yellow pods dangling from their trunks on thick stems. It looked like some trippy zeppelin docking station from a steampunk novel. People in canoes were poling through the forest, cutting the pods from the trees and piling them into their boats.

Volker gazed at them in awe as our dugout slipped into the trees. "Very impressive," he muttered to himself. In all his years at Baures and Tranquilidad, he'd never seen anything like it. This was no chocolatal. And these trees were clearly not remnants from somebody's ancient garden. They were truly wild, adapted perfectly to the seasonally flooded riverbanks.

He plucked a pod from a trunk and held it up to me. "No wild cacao? Bring them here! Show them this!" He laughed, smacked the side of the pod against the edge of the canoe, and twisted it open. Inside were dozens of white, maggoty-looking things. He held them out to me.

It was the first fresh cacao pod I'd ever seen. I stuck a handful of goop in my mouth. A sweet, lemony, delicious pulp came off the seeds. It was rich and tropical, like lychee, and I instantly understood why human beings had been idly sucking on these things for ten thousand years. Sitting there in the canoe in the strange understory light, tasting the juice and watching the boats gliding through the trees, I felt a first inkling of the reverberations cacao brings with it. It was as if we'd come unstuck in time.

I sucked seeds all the way to Combate. With a population of perhaps eighty people, Combate represented the largest settlement on this part of the river. It was key to Volker's vision. If he was going to harvest tons of cacao on the Mamoré, he was going to need their help.

A dozen thatch-roofed palapas came into view. The entire settlement was flooded, the palapas sticking up on posts. A sheet of brown water flowed across the compound, froth piling up where it met obstacles. Toddlers waded unsteadily through the current. Chickens perched on carts and stumps, trying to come up with plan B. Pet macaws clung to the mango trees.

We pulled up on the flooded bank next to a larger wooden boat festooned with children, who immediately piled onto our boat. They placed a tiny monkey on my shoulder and giggled.

The large boat had been commissioned by Volker for his Mamoré enterprise, built by local boatbuilders, and delivered by Francisco Brito—cacique, or chief, of the Yurucaré—who was standing on it conversing with some of the local men.

Francisco was a big guy with a big presence. He had his fingers in all sorts of forest enterprises. Logging, fishing, god knows what else. For years, he'd been trading food and gas to the people of Combate in exchange for cacao. Technically, it was his territory, so any deal Volker struck would have to go through Francisco, but it was up to Volker to pitch his plan and get everyone on board.

As the first step in their charm offensive, Francisco had arrived with a stack of cases of Colônia beer, a Brazilian brew smuggled across the border. Cans of beer didn't make it this far into the jungle very often. It was the tried and true way to get a party rolling. Unfortunately, Francisco had arrived a few hours before us. By the time we pulled up, the men of Combate were drooping from his boat like tree sloths.

A small, handsome man in his thirties with bloodshot eyes and a sailor's gait roused himself, stumbled over, and identified himself as Guillermo Figueroa, spokesman for Combate. He was wearing a green soccer shirt and jean shorts. "You're too late," he said unsteadily. "Today we drink. Tomorrow we'll meet." Then he grabbed a fresh six-pack and splashed off toward a hut with his buddies.

There was nothing to be done but crack open a couple of warm ones ourselves. We climbed aboard Volker's new boat. He christened it *Sundance*, in honor of Butch Cassidy and the Sundance Kid, who went down in a blaze of glory against the Bolivian police in 1908. This also didn't strike me as particularly auspicious, but I was new here. Volker lit a cigarette. Somebody handed me a bowl of fried piranha. We leaned into the lazy afternoon.

I watched the kids swimming in the river. The air was thick and humid, my skin caked with sweat and mashed mosquitoes. I asked if you have to worry about the piranhas. "Not this time of year," I was told. So I joined them, sticking to the shallows. The water was grainy with sand.

I dried off on *Sundance*, feeling much restored. Francisco's pet parakeet hopped onto my knee and squawked. His dog lay nearby, sporting a raw, curved wound across its head. The previous week, just upriver from Combate, a jaguar had approached Francisco's camp and the dog had lit out after it, nearly losing an eye in the fight. The dog escaped and Francisco immediately left the area, because once a jaguar and a dog have tussled, the jaguar will lie in wait to finish the job.

Volker sloshed around the settlement, examining the comical attempts to dry cacao in the Amazon during the rainy season. Beans were heaped anywhere that promised to stay out of the rising waters—canoes, huts, the crooks of trees. Some were getting nibbled by a coati. None of it was getting dry, and some of it was starting to germinate. Volker looked daunted by the task before him.

When evening arrived, we set up our hammocks on a platform in the middle of the settlement. They called it the church, though it consisted of nothing but a few planks and benches with a tin roof. The river flowed underneath. Beer cans and cacao pods floated past. Mosquitoes settled. The sky blushed all mango and papaya.

"Kitsch," Volker said, stubbing out another cigarette.

The light disappeared, and the din of frogs and insects filled the dark, punctuated by the occasional crazed peal of laughter from the hut of Combate men. If we were on the cusp of a chocolate revolution, it was certainly hard to tell.

10

Sundance

Beni, Bolivia, 2010

In the morning, Guillermo turned up looking surprisingly chipper. He whanged on an old piece of outboard with a metal pipe. If this was the church, then that, we supposed, was the bell.

An hour later, the only people who had assembled were Volker and me. Guillermo pounded on the metal again in frustration. Grudgingly, the rest of Combate joined us in the church. Guillermo and Volker made small talk as the others gathered. Why was the village called Combate? No one could remember, Guillermo said. Some trouble with another tribe.

I was the first person Guillermo had met from the States. When I told him coca was illegal there, he scrunched his eyebrows and shook his head in wonder.

Volker asked him if any of the children were his. Guillermo nodded proudly. "I have twenty-one children."

"Wow," Volker joked. "I guess the Church does say to go forth and multiply."

Guillermo scoffed. "No, they say we should stick to two or three."

"Then what happened?"

Guillermo smiled and shrugged. "I have no television." The crowd laughed and Guillermo basked in the attention.

Volker had already told me that he recognized the dynamics from his years of development work in other villages. There was always some dude who stole the stage and made a performance out of being in charge, but when it came to actually making decisions for the village's future, it generally fell to the women. He was really speaking to them.

And what he said was that the cacao growing up and down the Mamoré could make some of the best chocolate in the world. It could be worth a lot more money than it is now. But only if it's carefully fermented and dried. And right now, it isn't. Just look around.

We all glanced around at the fifty shades of rot currently on display. Nobody disagreed.

"If you work with me," Volker proposed, "I'll build a station where you can bring the cacao. Right here in Combate. I'll hire people from here to take care of it, and I'll teach them how. Aurelio will come every week in that boat to buy the cacao. *Every* week. And he'll bring food and gasoline."

Guillermo put his hand to his mouth in a shoveling motion. "We need food now. So how about you pay us now, and then you can come and get your cacao next year?"

Volker shook his head. No handouts. He was a business-person, not an NGO. He would pay a big premium for good cacao, and he would pay cash right here in Combate, but he couldn't pay in advance.

The crowd nodded. He'd passed the first test. Francisco said a few words in favor of the project, the meeting adjourned, and Volker broke out some paper and crayons and held a cacao-drawing contest for the kids, who had never played with a crayon before. They took to it like natural-born impressionists. Soon dozens of pages of golden pods and crazy cacao-tree people covered the benches, and we were all laughing hysterically.

And that turned out to be the real icebreaker. The women of Combate smiled at this goofy German drawing cacao monsters with their kids, and soon they and Volker were chatting away like old friends. To our surprise, they had no sentimental attachment to the cacao. It played no role in their culture. It was just another tree along the riverbanks. What they were very attached to, however, was their life on the river. If the cacao could help ensure that, they were all in.

Volker nodded in understanding. One mom tapped him on the shoulder with a final request. "Tell the cacique," she said, "next time, no more beer." He nodded again and said he'd make sure of it.

By the time we left Combate, things were looking good. A modicum of trust had been established, and both sides were happy with the prices. Now all Volker had to do was get the fermentation center built before next year's harvest and put the plan into action.

Sundance was about the size of a Boston Whaler, with a trellis roof covered by a blue tarp to block the punishing sun. The tarp didn't reach the back of the boat, so Dante threw a salted and butterflied pig carcass—our meat for the rest of the trip—over the top for shade. Whenever he stood up, he knocked his head on the dangling legs, sending droplets of sun-warmed fat cascading across the transom. The outboard had no casing and a number of jury-rigged parts. I was impressed at everyone's confidence in its ability to deliver us through three days of wilderness.

We bought all the cacao in Combate that wasn't rotten and stacked it in bags in the center of *Sundance*. The rest of the space was filled with backpacks, hammocks, piranha carcasses no one had cleaned up, a beer cooler, and bottles of water and gasoline, leaving nowhere to sit except the narrow gunwales— torture no amount of coca could disguise.

Our plan was to head downstream to Trinidad, stopping anytime we saw people with cacao. First up: the small settlements of Palermo and Jerusalem, Aurelio's childhood home. In Jerusalem, Aurelio and his brother had inherited a shack that bordered 7,500 acres of swampy rainforest rich in cacao. He was pretty sure the shack wasn't being used and we could spend the night there.

"First Palermo, then Jerusalem," Volker muttered darkly. "Sounds like a Crusade."

Cacao was everywhere along the river. We pulled up beside a woman opening a pile of pods with her machete and scooping the beans into a plastic bowl. Many of them were already rotten. Volker introduced himself and squatted at her feet to examine a rotten bean. "Señora," he said, "these are no good."

She shrugged in dismissal. "Somebody always buys them," she said.

He smiled. "If you separate these bad ones, you can get a higher price for the rest." She considered this momentarily, then shook her head. We moved on.

Another hour down the river, we found an old, shirtless man sitting outside a hut surrounded by well-manicured cacao trees. His name was Pedro, and he had lived there for forty-five years. He was the last of an Indigenous community of Moxeños people. Everyone else had moved to the city. He said there were 2,500 acres of cacao in the area, but there was no one left to harvest them.

I couldn't believe it. In other parts of the world, chocolate companies fought like hell over the paltry supply of high-grade cacao. Here, it rotted in the forest. My own tinkerer soul was starting to stir.

"What if I helped you get pickers during the season?" Volker asked Pedro. "And I provided food and training?" He nodded toward Aurelio. "And I send a boat every week? And we pay you a bonus for everything you harvest?"

"Why not?" said Pedro.

They shook on it.

Palermo was empty, abandoned to the floods. Who knew where the people had gone? We soldiered on, and after twelve back-breaking hours, we reached Jerusalem in the evening.

As soon as *Sundance*'s bow pushed into the soft mud in front of Aurelio's shack, I hopped off, thrilled to be freed from the boat. But then I stopped short. Every square inch of ground between the shore and the shack was covered in a thick carpet of composting cacao pods. Aurelio's brother and his family had been hard at work that week, opening pods and drying the beans in the shack. As I walked over the crunching pods, they seemed to be rippling. The entire grounds, even the floor of the shack, were alive with ants. They were swarming every surface, gorging on the sugary juice. And now they swarmed onto my legs and sunk their fire into me.

In the coming weeks, I'd be bitten by more creatures than I could count. Not the notorious ones. I got along famously with the caimans, piranhas, snakes, and tarantulas. And I never saw a jaguar, just some fresh tracks in the soft sand of a riverbank. But the mosquitoes turned my body into a vending machine of tropical microbes. Ticks buried themselves in my chest. Chiggers raised their rings of itch across my legs and hips and refused to die for weeks.

But the ants were the worst. They flow over the jungle floor in a pissy wave, killing small creatures in their way. They attack from the ground. They come boiling out of old wooden canoes. They even fall on you from the trees. They are the real lords of the jungle, and staying in the cabin with them would have been suicide. A year earlier, a drunken Bolivian farmhand had passed out against a palo santo tree, which is notorious for harboring ant nests in its honeycombed trunk. He never woke up. There have even been vigilante killings in Bolivia where suspected thieves were tied to palo santo trees and left for the ants.

We had to go somewhere else. But there was only an hour before dark. Dante, who had absorbed enough coca alkaloids over the course of the day to keep the city of Medellín partying for a week, voted for motoring blindly through the night. The rest of us overruled him.

"I have an idea," Aurelio said.

We puttered down an old, dead-end oxbow of the river as it turned purple, mirroring the sky. Pink river dolphins breached around us. Carpets of green dragonflies rippled over the water. Fireflies winked in the trees. Frogs trilled.

At the end of the lagoon, a single hut rose out of the water on stilts. Thatch roof, wooden floor, open sides. A gnarled couple stared as we approached, looking bewildered by the sudden turn their evening was taking.

The couple had been friends of Aurelio's parents. The man had lived on the river for sixty years and this was the highest water he'd ever seen. They graciously agreed to let us share their hut.

We were not the only ones. A box of piglets had been rescued from the flood and stashed inside. Their smoked predecessors hung from the rafters above. The six of us strung our hammocks in between and climbed in.

"It's rather aromatic in here," Volker said cheerily, reminiscing about the smoked sausages of his German youth. "Not unpleasant at all."

As the piercing squealiloquys stretched through the night, I struggled to sleep. A steady *whoosh* of air ruffled my face. When I switched on my headlamp, I saw hundreds of bats pinwheeling through the open hut, parting around my head like air over a plane wing. I shut off my headlamp and buried my face in the hammock mesh. Mr. Mosquito Coast snored contentedly beside me.

I had high hopes of making it back to Trinidad the next day—even a dingy hotel room with cold running water was starting to sound like decadence itself—but the banged-up outboard gave up the ghost midmorning. Any speed beyond a crawl produced a sickening thud with every rotation of the prop. We lashed *Sundance* to a tree on the bank, pulled the outboard onto the deck, and Dante and Aurelio grabbed their screwdrivers and proceeded to do the desperate and hopeless things that men do in such situations.

With the engine killed, the sounds of the jungle rushed in. One has this idea of the rainforest ringing with dulcet birdcalls, but for whatever reason, walking the rainforest is like making the rounds in a tuberculosis ward. The parrots screech. The macaws hack. The hoatzins sound like they could use a good exorcist.

Black cumulonimbus anvils approached from the west. I watched lightning flick between them. Howler monkeys roared from the banks, trying to outdo the thunder. I wondered how long we could all live on the bags of raw cacao beans.

The guys determined that the bushing that held our prop was shot, so our aluminum cooking pot was sacrificed to the cause. It took two hours to hacksaw a piece of metal out of it and bend it into a ring. It was an impressive display of MacGyverism, and for a moment, as Dante fired up the motor and we surged forward, my heart soared.

But in less than a minute, warmed by friction, the aluminum disintegrated like taffy, and we sloshed to a stop.

This time Dante just yanked up the outboard, threw it on deck, and stared as we drifted. Then he reached for his coca pouch.

Rain came sizzling up the river and lashed my face. Wind rocked the trees. The roaring on the banks closed in, as if the jungle itself were screaming in anticipation.

But we came up with plan C. Without the bushing, the engine could still be run at very low power—enough to steer, though not propel. And Aurelio's brother Angel lived just a few miles downstream from here, in the village of Camiaco. He could put us up for the night. Plus he owed us for the whole ant thing.

So we limped downstream at the river's pace, Dante just managing to keep us in the current. At nightfall, we dragged our soggy asses into Camiaco.

Angel had a little store on the river, a one-room wooden shack with basic items hanging from nails on the walls. We sat on plastic chairs on the sandy bank and watched a donkey stroll past. Volker fired up a cigarette. I gazed at the flowing water, trying to remember what my goals for the trip had been.

Meanwhile, Volker picked Angel's brain. "That was a lot of pods back at the shack," he observed.

"Yes," Angel said. "It's a good year. My guys are picking, but almost no one's buying."

Volker explained his situation.

Angel raised his eyebrows and swapped glances with Aurelio. "I can easily get you ten tons," he said. "Maybe more."

Volker put on his best poker face. "Every year?"

"Most years."

I'd been scanning the merchandise on the walls of the tiny store, and suddenly something clicked. "Do you sell chocolate?" I asked.

Angel disappeared and emerged moments later with a palm-sized lump of handmade chocolate. Its fragrant magic hit me from six feet away. After all the miles, the bugs, the rancid pork, I clutched it and held it close to my face, whimpering like Gollum with his ring.

Angel produced a tin cup of hot water and I crumbled half the lump into the liquid and stirred hard, trying to raise some froth. I sipped the rich brew, letting it seep into my cells. I began to feel a hell of a lot better.

"I'm pretty impressed," Volker chirped from his chair, cigarette in hand as we watched the Mamoré roll past. "It's much better than I thought. The volume of cacao from this river . . ." He raised his arms to indicate no estimate of such vast quantities was possible. He'd been doing thirty tons a year in Baures and environs, and it looked like he could double that on the Mamoré. Sure, sure, sure, he was getting ahead of himself. Logistics would be brutal. So would the fundraising. But . . . still. He was on the edge of something big.

I felt the same. The thoughts were still coalescing, but cacao was starting to feel less like a curiosity and more like a force. I blew a window in the foam and stared into the dark drink. Then I looked up at the brown river churning past, islands of foam spinning in the eddies. Then I leaned down into my chocolate and drank a cup of the Amazon.

What I didn't know was that like-minded people all over the world were also reconsidering what chocolate was and could be. We were part of a pattern, a new way of thinking that had been percolating for years in the chocolate underground. And, as these things do, it was ready to burst above the surface, seemingly everywhere at once. Chocolate needed to change. And it was time.

11

Big Chocolate

Belize, 2010 and 2022

There must have been something in the water in 2010," says Emily Stone. "Because at the same time that you were in the Amazon with Volker, and I was having these lightbulb moments, Dandelion Chocolate started. Dick Taylor Chocolate started. Ritual Chocolate started. And French Broad Chocolate started making bean-to-bar."

We're sitting in Simma Down, a wooden reggae bar in Punta Gorda, a run-down town on the coast of southern Belize. We're out on the deck, suspended over the bay by just a few nails that seem to be hanging on for dear life. You can see the blue mountains of Guatemala glimmering across the bay. There's cold beer and a stiff breeze off the water, which is finally taking the edge off the crushing heat of the day.

Emily is founder and CEO of Uncommon Cacao, the world's top importer of specialty cacao. She works directly with farmers and cooperatives around the world to buy their beans and get them into the hands of fine chocolate makers in Europe and the United States, providing a vital alternative to the commodity system. She's just reeled off a list of some of the greatest and most socially conscious chocolate companies in the world, which were all swimming in the same zeitgeist that I was in 2010, and she's explaining how that was also the year she had her epiphany, upended her life, and moved to Belize to join the cause, renting a dilapidated house just down the street.

"This is where I spent at least seventy percent of my nights and weekends when I lived here," she says, looking out over the water. "My best friends ran the place. It's where I'd come to think and to ponder the future. There's the beautiful ocean out there. The horizon. You can see storms coming in. You can see sunlight peeking through the clouds. It's always been a place where I found a lot of inspiration."

At the moment we could use a little inspiration, because it's been a tough day. We've been traveling the back roads of Belize in a thirty-three-year-old Ford F-250 with 289,000 miles, buying sacks of cacao from farmers Emily has been working with for years. And the big thing every one of them wanted to talk about was price. Although Maya Mountain Cacao, the company Emily started here in 2010, pays about twice the commodity price for cacao, the farmers said it wasn't enough. It was 2022, inflation was biting hard, and they needed more. And Emily had to tell them that she couldn't get them more . . . until she could start getting more from chocolate makers, who were already freaking out about *their* costs.

"It's really hard," she says. "Really hard. I want to change the world through this business. That's why I'm in this. Going through a day like today is emotionally exhausting for me, because so much of me wants to say, yes, we'll pay you whatever you need. We'll figure it out. And I made that mistake in the past, and it almost sank the business."

Being the middleman sucks. Your buyers always feel like they're paying too much. Your producers always feel like they're getting screwed. And you get all the blame. And ultimately, you're always competing with the capitalist hydra, which will find your markets through a thousand intermediaries and try to undercut you with cheap offerings.

And yet making those connections between producers and consumers and getting product to market is what makes every equitable food system possible. It's not sexy, but it's essential, and that's especially true for fine chocolate. You can be the most virtuous boutique chocolate maker in California, fully committed to working with small farmers and paying them a fair price, but how are you going to find those small farmers? How are you going to get their beans from the middle of nowhere, in a country you know nothing about, to your tiny factory? Are you up on your Ecuadorian customs regulations?

Everyone who's ever tried to change a system has run up against the daunting challenges of building a new one. The Felchlins and Valrhonas of the world can go to the trouble to export fifteen-ton shipping containers of cacao, but if the bean-to-bar revolution is going to grow, there have to be matchmakers to connect amazing tiny farms to amazing tiny chocolate makers.

Those are the challenges I've come to Belize to understand. What did it take to get this revolution started? And what's it going to take to keep it going? And Emily seemed like the perfect person to ask, because she had to figure it all out from scratch, starting from her own life crisis in 2010.

"You know," she says, wiping road grime from her forehead with the cold bottle, "I was bored as hell in my cubicle in Boston, not loving my life, working on these total deskwork campaigns and feeling like, 'Am I going in the right direction?'"

Emily was twenty-five, with several years as a community organizer under her belt. Smart and driven, with an easygoing manner and a ready smile, she was really good at rallying people to a cause. She'd been involved with Amnesty International since high school, and had been working for Green Century Capital Management as a shareholder advocate, pressuring publicly traded companies to do the right thing by helping them to see the risk in not. In other words, don't use those toxic chemicals in your packaging, or endanger your workers' health, because it's just going to come back to bite you in the bottom line.

It was valuable work, but spending all day drafting shareholders' resolutions on her computer was beginning to put her to sleep. "It wasn't satisfying my soul," she says. "I was really hungry for more creativity and entrepreneurship. You know, instead of just saying, 'Don't do this,' I wanted to come up with creative solutions."

That was when a new shareholder campaign against Hershey came across her desk. The goal was to pressure Hershey to get fair-trade certification for its entire cacao supply. And that sounded great to Emily. "I've loved chocolate since I was a little girl," she says. "I wrote a cookbook called *Desserts Around the World* for my first-ever independent school project."

So she dove right in. And she quickly learned that fair trade was not the answer. Fair-trade organizations charge farmers to be certified, and in many cases, a disturbing amount of the extra money raised by fair-trade products goes to support the fair-trade bureaucracy itself. Fair trade is better than nothing, but it has been found to deliver little extra income to cacao farmers, while burdening them with red tape and restrictions. It doesn't lift them out of poverty.

The more Emily learned about the chocolate industry, the more outraged she became. "I loved chocolate, and I just could not *believe* how little I knew about it! Ninety percent of the world's cacao is being produced by smallholder farming families, and over eighty percent of those families are living on under three dollars a day!"

Emily was horrified. "I was devastated to learn about all of these human rights and social issues in the supply chain of a product that I absolutely loved, and outraged that no one seemed to be doing anything about it. Chocolate is not a daily necessity. There's no reason for it to be causing poverty. It's the leftover inheritance of colonialism and of a world in which slavery was legal!"

I nod in agreement. She's hit on the disconnect that's been bugging me for years. How has a food that serves as a source of joy for so many people around the world been allowed to inflict grinding misery on millions of others?

There is an answer to that question, but it's not a simple one. It's tied up in the weird circumstances of how an American tree became an African industry, and how that industry came to be dominated—but, importantly, not owned—by the handful of multinational corporations collectively and pejoratively known as Big Chocolate.

In a sense, cacao's fatal flaw is that once dried, the beans last indefinitely. Stick them in a warehouse for a few years, they can still be ground into chocolate. That's what turned them into a currency in ancient times and a commodity in modern ones. And that means that every cacao bean is always competing with every other cacao bean on earth.

For most of history, that hasn't been much of a problem, because demand for the delicious nuggets exceeded supply. For farmers, they were a good crop to grow: decent prices, always a buyer. But they were also a tough crop to grow in their Latin American homelands, always beset by diseases and labor shortages.

No wonder European countries planted cacao in their West African colonies in the 1800s. The new high-yielding hybrid varieties thrived in the hot, humid climate, labor was abundant and criminally cheap, and the European markets were not too far away. Few people expected those colonies to do more than supplement what had always been a Latin American industry, but in the 1900s they shocked the world by taking over cacao production.

Ghana led the way. In 1892, it had never produced a cacao bean. Twenty years later, it was number one in the world, and by the 1920s it was producing two hundred thousand tons per year, more than the rest of the world combined.

This was not a top-down effort led by European planters. It was spearheaded by the Ghanaian farmers themselves, who saw an opportunity and went for it. Cacao was easy to grow on a few acres of land, it required little more than machetes and strong young backs, it could be sun-dried for transport, and it could always be turned into cash. After independence in 1957, the Ghanaian government bet hard on cacao as its path to economic prosperity. The young country had no money or infrastructure, but it had tons of land and a growing population in need of jobs. The government established relationships with international buyers, keeping a big chunk of the profits to fuel Ghana's development. As long as cacao prices remained high, times were good.

Ghana continued to be number one in the world until the 1970s, when its neighbor Ivory Coast surged past it. The cacao boom in Ivory Coast was even more extreme than the one in Ghana. With cacao prices at all-time highs, people in Ivory Coast's overcrowded towns and cities rushed to the forests—with the government's blessing—to clear a few acres of land and plant cacao. They were eventually joined by hundreds of thousands of refugees from neighboring countries like Mali and Burkina Faso, where economic and political conditions were so bad that working on a cacao farm, even for a dollar a day, was a vast improvement.

The land where these farms were being cleared was rainforest, much of it in ostensible preserves, but there was nobody to mind the store. Today, Ghana and Ivory Coast account for two-thirds of world production, a huge amount of it from supposed preserves, and their forests are essentially gone.

When this history is told in the media, cacao is often cited as the villain responsible, as though it wouldn't have happened if not for chocolate. But cacao was just the best option, the shelf-stable thing that millions of desperately poor people living in the tropical hinterlands could grow for cash. If not cacao, they would have planted the next best thing. The real villain was the market, and the fact that rich nations were happy to let these struggling young nations liquidate their natural and human capital at the lowest possible price.

What made the whole system possible was the century-long evolution of an extraordinary supply chain capable of getting those beans from West African fields to American grocery shelves. Emily Stone sketched it for me. A typical cacao farmer in the West African countryside can't afford a vehicle, so he sells his cacao for an absurdly low price to a local trader who has a truck. That trader collects from many farmers, then drives the cacao to the nearest city and sells to a cooperative, which in turn sells to an exporter in a port city. That exporter aggregates cacao from thousands of farms and sells it to international "grinders" like Cargill and Barry Callebaut that are in the business of moving huge volumes. Then it's loaded onto a freighter and shipped to warehouses in Europe.

Usually that transport happens in shipping containers, but not always, says Emily. "I've seen huge boats being unloaded with hundreds and hundreds of loose cocoa bags in the hold. And in some cases it's not even bagged! Beans are sucked up from the warehouse with a vacuum and just dumped into the ship. And then they're transported to warehouses in Amsterdam and Belgium, where they're sucked out of the boat and stacked up into these huge mountains of cocoa beans."

And there they sit, awaiting a buyer. Sometimes that buyer will be a famous chocolate brand, but most of the world's chocolate is made by the big grinders, then sold to retail chocolate makers like Hershey. There, the beans are roasted, winnowed, and ground into chocolate paste or chocolate "liquor"—liquid chocolate kept warm in heated tanks—as well as cocoa powder and cocoa butter, then mixed with sugar and other flavorings into different forms of "bulk chocolate." That's what gets sold to Big Chocolate, and Little Chocolate as well. And yes, that means that most chocolate companies that don't clearly identify themselves as bean-to-bar don't make their own chocolate. They buy it, remelt it, and pour it into cute molds with their logo stamped into them.

Emily says that a typical bean can pass through a dozen middlemen on its journey from farm to consumer, and few of these middlemen are keeping track of where each lot came from. Why would you? A bean is a bean. And they all melt into that $130 billion river we call chocolate.

If cacao prices had stayed as high as they were in the 1970s, things might have turned out better for Africa's farmers, if not its forests. But they didn't. In the 1980s, all those new Ivory Coast cacao farms began producing, flooding the market with a million tons a year. Prices plunged, never to recover.

And that's how we have the crazy situation today. Fifty million people, mostly in Africa, producing five million tons of cacao a year, and making on average about one dollar a day. Take it or leave it.

According to market dogma, what should happen is more farmers should leave it, switching to some other more profitable crop, until the cacao supply falls and prices rise. Unfortunately, most cacao is being farmed in regions mired in civil wars, with unstable governments, rogue militias, and minimal infrastructure. With no options, most farmers are forced to take it.

The way cacao farmers have made the impossible numbers work is to reduce their labor costs to near zero by putting their kids to work. About two million children work in Africa's cacao fields. Most of them are just putting in a few hours of chores before or after school, but a minority work full-time instead of going to school. In other cases, they are refugees fleeing neighboring countries, trafficked into cacao plantations and put to work in exchange for room and board and usually almost no pay.

Outrageous? Indeed, and people have been outraged for more than twenty years, ever since news stories first exposed the extent of the problem in the 1990s. In 2001, the outrage reached the U.S. Congress, when New York representative Eliot Engel introduced an amendment to a Food and Drug Administration appropriations bill that would have funded the development of a labeling system for chocolate products that would certify them as being produced without child slave labor—if companies could prove it. The amendment easily passed the House, and Iowa senator Tom Harkin championed the bill in the Senate, with little resistance.

In a panic, the industry lobbied desperately and ferociously, hiring former Senate heavyweights George Mitchell and Bob Dole to put a stop to it. They did. Instead of a labeling law, eight members of Big Chocolate—including Hershey, Mars, Nestlé, and Barry Callebaut—along with Harkin, Engel, and the ambassador of Ivory Coast, signed the Harkin-Engel Protocol, which called for producers to eliminate "the worst forms of child labor."

Unfortunately, the agreement was voluntary and nonbinding, with no consequences for failing to implement the new standards by the 2005 deadline, which was convenient for Big Chocolate, because even if it had been serious about eliminating child labor from the supply chain, it had no way to do so. Cacao was a strange industry. The companies with all the power were many layers of remove from the people producing the key product, and they liked it that way. Why take ownership of a business that was hopelessly unprofitable and morally problematic?

But the distance Big Chocolate maintained from its farmers also meant that it had very little control over or information about the origins of its cacao. An extra layer of complication was introduced by the corrupt governments of Ghana and Ivory Coast, which insisted that the business pass through them. They paid the farmers, and they didn't necessarily share the details of that arrangement with Big Chocolate.

In short, the fundamentals of the chocolate business were not so different from those of the cocaine business, and were equally hard to control. By 2005, the goals had not been met, and all parties agreed to a 2008 extension. In 2008, Big Chocolate agreed to keep working on it and to set up independent certification by 2010. In 2010, it changed the agreement to aim for a 70 percent reduction in the worst forms of child slavery by 2020. In 2020, it stopped pretending even that was possible. To be fair, the companies have made major efforts to improve the situation, but in spite of them, Big Chocolate still doesn't know where most of its cacao comes from. It just knows not to look too closely.

The more Emily Stone learned about the deep inequities of the cacao system, the more she wanted to take an active role in building an alternative. A vision started to emerge once she learned that cacao was an American thing, deeply rooted in the history of the Maya and other Indigenous cultures.

"Not once in my life had I seen a chocolate bar on a shelf that mentioned anything about Mexico, Guatemala, Honduras, Belize, or Central America," she says. "Not once!" But if there was a chance to free cacao from the hydra's jaws, it was probably going to come in the Americas, where Big Chocolate had less of a presence. And once she started thinking about it, she couldn't stop. "The gears just started turning. Like, 'Oh my god, this is what I was meant to do!'"

So she googled around until she found one of the few people who was actively doing something at that time. And as fate would have it, he was an easy T ride away in Somerville, Massachusetts.

On September 30, 2010, Emily walked into the Taza Chocolate factory and sat down for a meeting with its founder, Alex Whitmore. Whitmore was one of the pioneers of a system known as direct trade, which skips the middlemen and seeks to establish direct relationships with farmers. He wanted Taza to use high-quality organic chocolate, and wanted to pay small farmers a premium to source it. But he was finding it nearly impossible. There was simply no supply chain set up to deliver such a product. The commodity system ruled.

Whitmore mentioned Belize as an example. Many Maya farmers in the country were growing organic cacao, but there was no organization, no centralized processing, zero quality control, and wildly inconsistent flavor. Short of flying down there, buying and fermenting the beans himself, and flying them home, he had no way of getting the cacao he needed, much less helping the farmers.

"So there was this big missing middle," Emily says. How to fix it? Well, you could set up a new company in Belize to take care of all the logistics . . . if you had someone crazy enough to take that on . . .

Emily laughs as she recalls the pivotal moment in her life. "And he was like, 'Do you want to go to Belize? Do you want to try to run the thing?' And I was like, 'HELL YES!'"

She gave her notice that day. A month later, she flew to Belize with a mission . . . and no idea how to pull it off.

The Legend of Chocfinger

In 2010, the same year that Emily Stone was getting started on her new career path, the world of Big Chocolate was thrown into a tizzy by a London commodity trader known as Chocfinger. Chocfinger's real name is Anthony Ward. A longtime expert in cacao markets, he'd earned his moniker in 2002 when he tried to buy enough cacao to corner the market and control the price—as his namesake, the Bond villain Goldfinger, had tried to do with the world's gold supply.

It hadn't worked for Chocfinger in 2002—he wasn't able to accumulate enough beans to jolt the global price—but in 2009 he tried again with more firepower. He had intel in Africa, and he'd heard that the harvest was going to be light because of bad weather. So he pounced, purchasing a futures contract on 241,000 tons of cacao at a price of about three thousand dollars per ton.

A futures contract is an agreement to buy a commodity at a later date at an agreed price. If the price goes up, the trader makes money by buying at the agreed price and selling at the new, higher price. If it goes down, he has to unload his contracts at a loss. That kind of trade happens every day. What was different about this one was the size. Together with some other futures contracts he signed, Chocfinger had committed a billion dollars to buy one seventh of the entire 2010 cacao supply, enough to make more than *five billion* candy bars.

And it looked like it was going to pay off brilliantly. By mid-2010, when Chocfinger's futures contracts came due, the price of cacao had risen to nearly four thousand dollars per ton. He was going to make hundreds of millions of dollars on his trade. Everyone tipped their hat. *Nice move, Chocfinger.*

But this is where Chocfinger surprised us all. Commodities traders are basically keyboard jockeys, buying and selling from their laptops. They move pixels around, not goods. Prices go up and down, people make money and lose money, but the flow of beans continues unimpeded. And that is what everyone expected to happen this time. Chocfinger would buy the beans at three thousand dollars and sell them almost instantaneously for a handsome profit.

But Chocfinger didn't sell. Instead, he said, "Send me the beans." And that's when everyone freaked out. More than fourteen percent of the world's cacao, shipped to warehouses in Europe, off the market. Suddenly every chocolate company worried that it wouldn't be able to get enough chocolate for the holidays. The price of cacao soared to a thirty-year high, and chocolate companies wrote furious letters to the trade commissions complaining about market manipulation.

It didn't actually work for Chocfinger this time, either. He held his beans too long, the price of beans mysteriously tanked, he lost a lot of money, and soon it was Chocfinger complaining about the opaque workings of the market. What L'Affaire Chocfinger really showed was how damaging the commodities game is for the regular human beings in the system who are actually trying to grow stuff or make stuff, all of whom benefit from a stable, predictable price.

But the spirit of Chocfinger lives on, as recent developments have made clear. In 2020, Ivory Coast and Ghana, the two biggest cacao producers by far, introduced a living-income differential of four hundred dollars that would be added to the price of every ton of cacao they sold and passed directly to the farmers, who were currently making seventy-eight cents per day on average. All the big companies agreed to the surcharge, but shortly after, rumors swirled of a mysterious buyer who had prepurchased 30,000 tons of cacao on the futures exchange before the surcharge could kick in. According to media reports, that secret somebody was Hershey. The company was pilloried in the press for the move, but as some experts pointed out, it was basic business.

Shortly after that, Covid-19 hit, and demand for cacao withered. Prices plunged as traders tried to unload their beans, and farmers once again struggled to survive. But by 2023, things had shifted. Two years of terrible harvests in West Africa due to drought and disease outbreaks had left supplies the tightest they'd been in forty years, and once again buyers were scrambling to secure enough beans. Cargill, the largest crop trader in the world and the second-largest processor of cacao, after Barry Callebaut, pulled a Chocfinger move of its own, scooping up 140,000 tons of cacao and squirreling it away in its warehouses, which only drove prices all the higher, surpassing the Chocfinger-driven 2010 peak and reaching numbers not seen since 1977.

Then, in 2024, true insanity took hold, as yields in West Africa once again tanked and the true costs of grinding prices as low as they could go came back to bite the industry. With no money to maintain the health of their groves, farmers production plunged for the third year in a row, decimated by diseases and bad weather, and a shortfall (the gap between demand and supply) of 500 million tons by far the largest in history—panicked all players. Prices rose to $6,000 per ton in February and kept on rising, blowing past the 1977 record high of $7,700 in March and continuing to explode, surpassing $10,000 per ton in April and showing no signs of coming back down.

It's clear that the reckoning the industry has long hoped to avoid is at hand, and the era of cheap chocolate may be over forever. And that's just fine. It may be terrible news for Big Chocolate, but one beneficiary of these trends could be the people working with wild and heirloom cacao in Latin America, whose fine-flavor beans may start to look more and more like great bargains—as they always were.

12

Stranded Assets

Belize, 2010

The airport in Punta Gorda, the closest thing southern Belize has to a town, is a strip of concrete with a one-room shack beside it. Back in 2010, it didn't even have a fence around it. The local goats just knew to scatter when they heard a plane coming in.

That November, the puddle jumper from Belize City landed just long enough to discharge a single passenger on an unpaid scouting mission. Emily Stone's agreement with Alex Whitmore was that she would spend a few months checking out the scene, figuring out if there was any way to boost the quality and reliability of the organic cacao supply. If it looked like there was a path, then they would launch a new company together, with Taza Chocolate buying whatever they could produce.

Most of the people living in southern Belize are Maya, close relatives of the Maya right across the border in Guatemala. Most families always grew a little cacao as part of their heritage, just enough to make drinking chocolate for ceremonies and harvest festivals, but never for export. But things changed in the late 1970s, when Hershey gambled big on Belize.

Like the other members of Big Chocolate, Hershey had always kept a healthy distance between itself and the people growing its primary ingredient. Both chocolate and cacao were easily sourced from a thousand middlemen. Why lose money farming it?

Now Hershey reconsidered. Demand for cocoa was surging, but supply wasn't keeping up. When West Africa suffered a couple of years of bad crops, the price of cocoa spiked from about $600 per ton in the early 1970s to $5,700 per ton in 1977. Hershey was getting killed. If prices kept exploding, it would actually save money by producing its own supply. (Had the company known that the price of cacao wouldn't reach such eye-watering heights for forty-six years, it might have reconsidered.)

Since Belize had a perfect climate and America-friendly politics (it was still part of the U.K. at the time), plus a culture of cacao-growing due to its Maya heritage, Hershey decided it was the best place to run its experiment. It bought 500 acres of land on the Hummingbird Highway and launched a cacao farm and harvest center that came to be known as Hummingbird Hershey. Soon it expanded to 1,800 acres. Hershey struck an agreement with the government to buy all the cacao Belize could grow at the market price. Its extension agents, in tandem with USAID, fanned out through the Maya communities of southern Belize, teaching modern farming and fermentation techniques and providing the seedlings and equipment to do it.

Times were good, and the Maya farmers made the best of it. Soon several hundred of them were growing cacao and selling to Hershey. Acreage expanded from two hundred to over a thousand. It was never more than a drop in the bucket of Hershey's annual usage, but the company seemed satisfied with the arrangement. And though prices quickly dropped from the stratospheric heights of the late 1970s, down to $2,000 to $3,000 per ton through the '80s, that was still plenty to make a better living than most of them had ever made in their lives. It felt too good to be true. And it was.

In the 1990s, Ivory Coast cacao glutted the market, and the price crashed right back to $1,000 per ton, the cheapest in decades. Once again, farming cacao looked like a losing venture, and in 1993 Hershey pulled out of Belize with head-turning speed. Hummingbird Hershey was sold and converted to an orange plantation, and the Maya farmers were left with no buyer.

But amazing and unlikely salvation was right around the corner. A new U.K. chocolate maker called Green & Black's launched in 1991, the first to focus on organic chocolate. Green & Black's was hungry for reliable, tasty cacao supplies, and it liked what it saw in Belize. In 1993, the company swooped in, funding the farmers' transition to organic production and certification, and buying all the cacao Belize could make at more than double the commodity price. Happy days!

This time, the good times lasted about a decade. Then, in 2005, Green & Black's was bought by Cadbury, which was soon acquired by Kraft Foods, which soon became part of Mondelēz International, one of the world's largest food corporations. The megacompany quickly severed its ties to Belize and returned to buying cacao on the world exchange, and again the farmers were left high and dry, burned twice by the international market.

So in 2010, when a young American woman with big ideas showed up, they didn't exactly jump for joy.

Emily Stone rented a crumbling house on a run-down lane on the Punta Gorda waterfront with a drop-dead view of the ocean and got to work. As a stranger in a strange land, she knew better than to impose her ideas on a place she barely understood. So she began with a listening tour. She took the local buses from village to village, walking around, asking questions, knocking on the doors of as many cacao farmers as she could, learning how things worked and what could work better.

And what she learned was astonishing. Since Green & Black's had pulled out, the system had collapsed. Belize barely had a functioning cacao industry at all. The farmers lived on remote hill farms with no vehicles. After harvesting their cacao, it was up to them to ferment and dry it at home. They had no facilities for doing this, so that usually meant the fermentation was spotty and the drying was done on a tarp in the sun, with hopes that somebody in the family would keep the chickens from pooping on the beans. If rain came, hopefully someone was around to drag the tarp under cover. Quality was all over the map.

And even if the beans were successfully dried, the adventure had just begun. The only place to sell cacao was a single buying station in Punta Gorda, and it was open only on Saturdays. So once a week, the farmers would load their dry cacao into buckets and sacks, get on a bus, bring it to the buying station, and stand in line. Sometimes the buying station ran out of cash. Sometimes their cacao got rejected for being moldy. When that happened, they had to haul the cacao back home on the bus and literally eat it themselves. Even when they did manage to sell their cacao, prices were barely high enough to cover costs. Many were giving up on cacao altogether.

For Emily, that was exactly the kind of win-win opportunity she was looking for. The farmers' needs were clear. They needed a better way to ferment and dry their beans. They needed a better way to get them to market. And they needed to know they would get paid a decent price.

These were all things she could provide. Raise a little capital, buy a truck, build a fermentation center. The costs would be covered by the high price that organic, well-fermented beans would receive. If she ever managed to produce more than Taza could use, the burgeoning bean-to-bar scene in the United States would snap it up.

Emily was painfully aware of her privilege—she had access to U.S. markets and U.S. capital, and the locals didn't—but it was what she had to offer. So she made her pitch. She said, Look, here's a better idea. I'll buy your cacao from you, fresh. You just pick the pods, bag the beans, and I'll come by with a truck and pay you cash—on the spot. You don't have to worry about fermenting and drying. No more buckets and buses. More money for you, less worry.

In a sense, it was not so different from the deal Volker Lehmann was offering harvesters in the Amazon—except the trees weren't wild, no boats were involved, and no remote drying would be necessary. That eliminated most of the chaos. It seemed like a slam dunk. What farmer wouldn't take Emily up on her offer?

Well, a lot, as it turned out.

"There has to be so much trust between cacao producers and cacao buyers for any of this work," Emily tells me from the deck of the Punta Gorda reggae bar during our 2022 visit. "I came in as a naive twenty-five-year-old, idealistic white girl with this big vision to make an impact and change the world. And I got burned real fast with that mindset. I thought, I'm going to sit down with these farmers, they're all going to sign up, and it's going to be great. And what I heard over and over again was, 'We don't trust you. We've had so many gringo entrepreneurs just like you come to our village and say they're going to buy our product, whether it's cacao or annatto or allspice or rice, and make all these promises, and then leave us in the dust.' It had left a lot of them really jaded, for good reason."

Rural Central America is also a pretty conservative place, and the farmers didn't know what to make of this single white woman in her ball cap and Tevas trying to buy their cacao. "I would ask people on my team, 'What are people saying about me? Like, what's the word on the street?' And what I heard was that I was basically considered this genderless alien, because I didn't fill the traditional gender roles of either the man or the woman."

For months, farmer after farmer gave the genderless alien a polite no. It looked like her plan might not work after all. No one was willing to trust an outsider.

But after yet another fruitless meeting with a farmer, the son of the farmer followed her out the door. His name was Gabriel Pop, and he'd been to Costa Rica and Honduras and seen how farmers sell wet cacao in those countries. And he told Emily she was right. "He was like, 'Listen, I know what you're talking about. I know our model stinks. And I really want to help you make this work. But the way you're doing it right now is not going to work, because yes, we speak English in Belize, but we're Maya, and we mostly speak Kekchi and Mopan. And unless you start listening in Kekchi and Mopan, you're gonna miss what everyone really thinks. So I'm gonna be your translator. And I refuse to let you pay me, because I don't want anyone to think that I'm just being paid by the white person who's here to convince farmers of something. Let's get to work.'"

Having Gabriel on board changed everything. The people knew who he was, and he explained things in their native tongue. "It was absolutely incredible," Emily says. "He would take my ideas and translate them so farmers could really understand the vision and the model and give us real feedback. And after a couple months of those meetings, Gabriel was like, 'Listen, I think this is gonna work. I think we've got enough support. You can start paying me now.'"

Gabriel became a cofounder of the company, which they called Maya Mountain Cacao. They bought a truck, built a facility, and went into business. And the more farmers saw them coming through, paying the prices promised and paying up front, the more they signed up.

"I remember our first weekend buying, we bought sixty pounds of wet cacao from three different producers," Emily says. "And it felt like such a victory. I was like, 'Oh my god, people are excited about this! This is gonna work!' Fast-forward to today, we're buying sixty thousand pounds of cacao in a weekend."

Soon there was a two-year waiting list among bean-to-bar chocolate makers in the States for the distinctive honey-tobacco notes of Maya Mountain's premium organic beans. Prices doubled. And the Belize cacao industry tripled, from 40 tons per year to 120 tons, 90 of that from Maya Mountain.

But of course, 90 tons is a drop in the bucket of Big Chocolate's 5 million tons per year. Emily says she knew Maya Mountain could never be more than that. "It was really the pilot. The proof of point. Like, okay, cool, we can do this. We can make this happen. But the opportunity is so much bigger, and the need is so much bigger."

By 2013, the bean-to-bar chocolate market had exploded in the United States, from just a handful of companies a decade earlier to hundreds. Demand for high-quality beans was off the charts, more than Maya Mountain could ever supply. It was time to grow.

Emily takes a swig of her beer and looks out over the water, remembering her next big decision point. "I was right here, just like this, looking over this exact same vista." And what she was staring at was the twinkling lights of Guatemala, across the bay. "I was hearing from people in Belize, like, 'Oh yeah, my cousins in Guatemala have cacao. Have you ever been to Guatemala?' And I hadn't."

Guatemala produced a hundred times more cacao than Belize. The opportunity for impact was much larger. Unlike in Belize, almost no one spoke English, but Emily knew Spanish, from a homestay in Honduras when she was in high school, and by then she'd even taught herself a little Kekchi. "I knew that the cacao producers there were Kekchi, and I knew enough Kekchi to be able to explain what I was trying to do and ask some questions and understand some of their answers. So I felt prepared."

It would not take long for that feeling to disappear.

13

Verapaz

Alta Verapaz, Guatemala, 2013

In 2013, Emily Stone walked down the public pier in Punta Gorda, Belize, stepped onto the converted fishing skiff that served as the once-a-day ferry to Guatemala, found a seat beneath the plastic tarp rigged for shade, and made the forty-five-minute run across Amatique Bay to Puerto Barrios, the blue mountains of Guatemala slowly coming into focus.

Emily was headed for Alta Verapaz, the volcanic highlands of central Guatemala, sometimes dubbed the Guatemalan Alps for their high peaks and jaw-dropping views. She was hoping to re-create the success of Maya Mountain Cacao in Guatemala. She knew that the valleys of Alta Verapaz were hot spots of cacao production, but that was all she knew. She didn't know a single person in the country. But she'd made one contact by phone. As her tiny ferry pulled into Puerto Barrios, she just had to hope that she could find the guy, and that something good would happen from there.

Back in Belize, Emily had found a list of names and numbers of cacao producers from a training session that had been run in Guatemala a few years earlier. So she started cold-calling. No answer, no answer, and then finally, a guy picked up. His name was Francisco, and he was part of a farmers' association of Maya that grew chilies, cardamom, cinnamon . . . and cacao. "And I was like, 'Hey, my name's Emily! I work in cacao in Belize, and I'm interested in learning about the cacao industry in Guatemala. I'm looking to meet some producers.' And he was like, 'Yes, come. You can stay with me.'"

Score! Francisco lived in a tiny village called Pinares, way up in Alta Verapaz. The region had been a center of cacao farming since prehistoric times. In fact, it was responsible for the first cacao ever sent to Europe. In 1544, a delegation of Kekchi Maya from the Guatemala highlands accompanied the Dominican friar Bartolomé de Las Casas on a journey across the Atlantic to visit the Spanish court. Las Casas was a strong advocate for the rights of Indigenous groups in the Americas, and he hoped that a direct meeting between Maya and Spanish nobility, along with a display of Maya culture, would make an impression. One of the gifts the Kekchi brought with them was cacao. But the Spanish nobles showed much less interest in the strange beans than in the two thousand quetzal feathers. Now, almost five hundred years later, maybe Alta Verapaz cacao would have its moment.

But getting there from Puerto Barrios? Emily had to piece it together, one step at a time. "You know, anytime I got to the next bus station, just kind of asking around, like, 'Okay, how do I get from here to here?'"

Slowly, she found her way, town to town. El Rancho to Cobán. Cobán to Cahabón. From Cahabón, she needed the minibus to Pinares. Buses in Central America mostly aren't centralized in a public bus station. Every operator has its own garage. So she asked around town and finally found the spot. The bus was there, so she popped her head in and greeted the driver. "And I'm like, 'Hey, I need to go to Pinares. When do you leave?' And he kind of looked at me funny . . . And it was at that point that I turned my head . . . and saw bloodstains all over the back of this minibus." On the drive that morning from Pinares down to Cahabón, someone had been stabbed, and the driver was cleaning it up. "So I turned back to look at him. And he said, 'One o'clock.' And I was like, 'Great! I'll be here. One o'clock.'"

And she was. As the minibus switchbacked up the precipitous roads that afternoon, Emily wondered what she was getting herself into. But she didn't have too much time to think about it. The bus was packed with locals who were less thrown by the blood-soaked seats than by her. "Everyone's looking at me like, who the fuck are you? Are you a missionary? Are you a Jehovah's Witness? Someone asked me, 'What are you doing?' And I said, 'I'm here to meet with Francisco. I'm here to look at cacao.' And all of a sudden, they were like, 'Cacao! We have a lot of cacao!' And literally as the minibus was making its way up the mountain, we were stopping at every single person's cacao farm and getting out to admire the pods."

The cacao looked great. It was all old-school, fine-flavor varieties that hadn't been seen in decades. She couldn't imagine why, but as she asked questions, she began to figure it out. It turned out that in the 1980s, the president of Guatemala had launched a program to plant hundreds of thousands of seedlings of Guatemala's most prized cacao varieties on farms around the region, where he was from. But then time moved on, Guatemala fell on hard times, and the farmers and their cacao were forgotten. They were selling it cheap into the Mexican market for lack of options.

Emily stayed at Francisco's house, sleeping in a hammock beside his family members, communicating in a jumble of Spanish and Kekchi, doing cut tests on the beans on an overturned stool by the light of her headlamp to check quality. In the following days, as word got out about the American cacao woman, everyone in the community turned up to show Emily their beans.

It was all lavado, or washed. Not fermented at all. That's typical in Mexico and Guatemala, where almost all cacao is used in supersweet drinking chocolate. The good flavors produced by the fermentation process would just be masked by the sugar, and the astringency that would be ameliorated by fermentation is actually desired to offset the sweetness. So why bother with all the trouble of fermentation? Just open your pods, wash the pulp off the beans, and dry them as fast as possible.

For the farmers of Alta Verapaz, it had always been the right move. No one would have paid them more for finely fermented beans. In fact, the only buyers were coyotes—freelancers who drive their trucks through the back roads of Latin America with a stack of cash, a handgun, and a scale, buying whatever the farmers have to sell. They are the only game in town, and they dictate the price.

"I was so pumped!" Emily says. "It was one of those YEAH moments!" Some of the finest cacao to be found, being sold for pennies for lack of technical assistance, fermentation facilities, and market access. She could make a real difference.

Within the year, Emily launched a new company in Guatemala called Cacao Verapaz. She provided training in cultivation and fermentation, offered farmers twice the going rate for their cacao, and lined up buyers in the United States.

There was just one problem. The coyotes. They were not thrilled about losing their monopoly to a gringo do-gooder, and they pressured farmers not to sell to her. "It's been a huge challenge," Emily admits. "There were physical threats made to association members."

Emily shakes her head thinking about it. "It did reach a stage where we weren't allowed to come into the community. One coyote and his family members were like, 'If those people come, it's not going to be good.'" When Emily and the Guatemalan government teamed up to build a new fermentation and drying center for the community, the coyote spread rumors that they were secretly plotting to turn the area into a giant hydroelectric site.

Things reached a head when government representatives showed up at a ceremony to sign the paperwork, and the coyote was waiting for them. "Basically, this disgruntled guy and his family surrounded the building where the signing was happening, armed with machetes, and threatened that if they signed it, there would be violence. And so they left without signing. And the project never happened."

For several years, it was too dangerous for Emily to show her face in the area. But the benefits to the community were just too great. Farmers that sold to Cacao Verapaz profited handsomely from the higher prices and reliable business. Coyotes found it harder and harder to find any cacao to buy. And ultimately, they gave up.

Cacao Verapaz became the toast of American chocolate makers, just like Maya Mountain had, though Emily admits it still has to deal with the risks of rural Central America. "There have been instances of coffee containers being robbed violently in Guatemala, and obviously we want to ensure that our cacao does not get stolen on its way to port. So anytime we're shipping containers out, we have a security car with two armed guys following our container from the warehouse to the port."

In 2016, Emily again decided to expand the impact by growing her business. She launched Uncommon Cacao, which now imports fine-flavor beans from farmer cooperatives in a dozen countries, representing seven thousand farmers, and gets them into the hands of hundreds of bean-to-bar chocolate makers in the United States and Europe. Uncommon Cacao pays well above market rates, but its most radical move has been to introduce what it calls "transparent trade." In its annual *Transparency Report*, Uncommon Cacao publishes the prices it pays to every producer, along with the average price it sells the beans for. For the first time, farmers don't have to rely on coyotes, unscrupulous traders, or Big Chocolate to tell them what their labor is worth.

It's not all perfect. Industry insiders sometimes criticize Uncommon Cacao for not paying its farmers more, but at some level, the company is always competing with commodity cacao. Chocolate makers have to care greatly about flavor and equity to pay huge premiums for specialty beans—especially now that prices have risen so drastically.

But it's working. For the first time, any new chocolate maker that wants to divorce itself from the commodity system, and work directly with a specific farm, is able to. Not only does that put more money into the hands of farmers; it also opens up new possibilities for improving chocolate. Most farmers never know what happens to their beans after they send them to market. Most have never tasted chocolate made from their cacao. If chocolate makers can close the loop with farmers, they can provide feedback on how the variety or the processing affects the chocolate. They can start chasing new flavors. They can make new connections between chocolate and place. They can redis-cover its spirit.

14

Remembrance of Chocolates Past

Salt Lake City, Peru, Belize, 2012–16

C lose your eyes and think about the most important flavors from your childhood. The ones that still trip your emotions. The ones that helped to form your impressions of the world and the things it contained. What were those flavors? Where did they come from? And why did they captivate you?

For Matt Caputo, the foods that formed him came from his Greek grandmother. "She had a tiny little plot in Salt Lake City," he remembers. "It was probably a tenth of an acre. She had two peach trees, two almond trees, two cherry trees, and two quince trees. She grew her own potatoes, dandelion greens, amaranth, and all sorts of herbs and vegetables. But these weren't seeds bought from the regular seed store. Almost all of them were starts or seeds that she brought with her from

Greece. So we had these really off-the-beaten-path flavors in our diet when I was a kid."

Matt admits that wasn't necessarily a positive thing for him at the time. "You know, I'd have friends come over, and here we are eating dandelion greens, and I'd be sitting there thinking, *Oh god, please don't recognize this stuff.* And for the most part, they didn't. But one time, my friend said, 'Are these weeds?' And I said, 'No! No, they're not.' And he said, 'Yes they are! These are dandelions!' And I was like, *Oh god.*"

But he got over it. As he grew up, he came to appreciate how those foods had broadened his horizons. "What I always remember is these flavors! Just the smell of my Yaya's kitchen during the summer when everything was laid out on the counters. Just . . . *her* food, you know? Her food didn't taste like anything else. Her produce didn't taste like the produce you buy in the grocery store. So I became accustomed to looking for flavors that don't really exist in what has become a pretty monoculture food system. And that has been really formative for me."

Taste and smell are some of the most important ways that we make meaning of our daily experience. They are the building blocks. Matt's job at Caputo's required him to taste widely, and the more he did, the more he realized that some building blocks had a lot more character than others. "There's food as simple sustenance that keeps you alive, and there's food that connects you to this communal past we all share. I love feeling like the things that I consume can mean more than just keeping me alive. And I don't just mean my Greek grandmother. No matter where you're from in the world, you have beautiful traditions, delicious foods, incredibly rich ingredients. And I think it's important that we hold on to some of these really beautiful things."

Matt turned Caputo's into a showroom for those taste experiences and the cultures behind them. But over the years, he watched in dismay as those authentic flavors began disappearing. "Over the course of my career, I'd see that it was harder and harder to get a raw-milk Pecorino Romano. They started to taste different. They just weren't the same. And I'd see this trajectory in every category, not just cheese. Things getting more and more homogenized, more and more flavorless."

That's been a long-term trend in every segment of the food system, as small-scale producers get beaten down on price and squeezed out by the industrial system and its economies of scale. Efficiency leads to sameness and lack of character as everything that was quirky or rare or just plain different gets ironed out of the system.

And as people become exposed to fewer flavors—when they never taste the dandelion greens—their experience of the world gets narrower and narrower. And as we lose these small-scale artisans who saw their creations as manifestations of that world in all its beauty, we lose the world as well.

"At some point it just crystallized," says Matt. "We need to fight to preserve the food traditions of our ancestors. Not just because of flavor, not just because of tradition, not just because of culture, but because this type of food tends to intrinsically support other things we care about, like biodiversity, sustainability, and social and economic justice. So we've kind of made it everything we do at Caputo's."

By the early 2010s, Matt and others in the fine chocolate business were fearful of the same winnowing of diversity in the

world of cacao. For every Cru Sauvage to appear, there were
dozens of small farmers replacing their aging cacao trees with
modern hybrids, or simply abandoning their farms to the jungle.

And then, in 2012, a unique and quirky nonprofit formed to
stop the hemorrhaging: the Heirloom Cacao Preservation Fund.

By 2012, both chocolate experts and U.S. Department of Agriculture researchers had independently begun worrying that cacao
was heading for some sort of genetic bottleneck. It was the
USDA's job to worry about the genetics of any crop essential to
U.S. food production, and what its researchers were finding was
that, as with so many other crops, the industry had settled on
just a handful of closely related and interbred hybrids with very
little genetic diversity. Those monocrops worked great—until the
right disease came along and wiped them out. Resistance to
future diseases probably could be found in some of those heirlooms from cacao's preindustrial past, as well as in the wild
strains, but both of these reservoirs were disappearing fast.

These concerns had come to a head a few years earlier, when
one USDA researcher on a collecting expedition in the Brazilian
Amazon had come across a cacao tree with blue pods. Cacao
pods can be green, orange, red, yellow, even purple, but no one
had ever seen a blue one. The researcher excitedly tagged the tree
on his GPS and returned the following spring to study it and
look for more, only to find that the entire section of forest
containing the tree had been razed for soybean fields. No one
has seen a cacao tree with blue pods since.

For members of the Fine Chocolate Industry Association, the
issue was flavor. Yes, a handful of great heirlooms like Chuao
were high in demand and in no danger of disappearing, but for

every Chuao, there were a dozen unknown heirlooms on the brink of oblivion, and no one was actively saving them.

So the two groups came together to launch the Heirloom Cacao Preservation Fund, or the HCP, with the goal of identifying the world's great cacaos and bringing them to the market's attention. That way, the thinking went, they would command a high price and would continue to be grown and preserved.

The event that directly precipitated the formation of the HCP was a perfect example. In 2009, an American man named Dan Pearson and his stepson were provisioning mining companies in Peru's remote and rugged Marañón Canyon. There, they discovered farmers still growing a white-beaned cacao, and alerted the USDA, which tested the beans and determined them to be pure Nacional, the prized ancient variety of Ecuador, thought to have disappeared in the 1920s when it was ravaged by disease and replaced with modern hybrids.

Today, Nacional is again in high demand and is being grown by small farmers in Peru and Ecuador. It's even the source of the most expensive chocolate bar on earth, a 100 percent ancient Nacional bar made by To'ak that originally sold for $365 per bar but now can be had for closer to $50. To'ak funnels the money into a nonprofit that has planted thousands of Nacional seedlings in Ecuador and reforested entire hillsides.

But how many other quality cacaos were out there, hiding in the jungle, one new cattle ranch away from extinction? Pearson teamed up with Pam Williams, the founder of the Vancouver chocolate-making school Ecole Chocolat, and other experts from the world of chocolate to launch the Heirloom Cacao Preservation Fund.

The HCP set up a remarkably rigorous protocol for identifying worthy candidates. Any cacao producer in the world can submit a sample of beans to the HCP for consideration. San Francisco's 150-year-old Guittard Chocolate Company, one of the HCP's founding members, roasts the beans and makes the chocolate in its test lab, then distributes blind samples for evaluation to the HCP's tasting panel, nine of the world's most exacting chocolate experts. Without sharing their impressions with other panelists, each member gives the sample a score of 1 to 10 for overall flavor and uniqueness of flavor, and votes yes or no for heirloom designation. To achieve heirloom status, a sample must get a thumbs-up from a supermajority of more than 70 percent of the panel.

Most samples don't make the cut, but the few that do are sent to the USDA for genetic analysis. If the USDA determines the beans to be genetically distinctive—in other words, not something that's already widely available from multiple sources—then it gets certified by the HCP as an heirloom, hopefully drawing the attention of bean-to-bar chocolate makers. Matt Caputo loved the idea so much that he joined the board and became a major supporter, donating the proceeds of the annual chocolate festival Caputo's throws in Salt Lake City.

The first HCP designee was a no-brainer: Volker Lehmann's Beniano beans from Bolivia. Soon others were added, including Emily Stone's Maya Mountain Cacao and an ancient Nacional variety from Ecuador's Piedra de Plata valley.

In 2015, Jacob Marlin got wind of the HCP and began wondering how his wild Belize beans might fit in. He knew that the unusual white color of the beans meant they were probably part of the Criollo family, but all the other Criollos in circulation were actually a hodgepodge of different cacao strains, Criollo mixed with other stuff. He assumed his would be the same.

Jacob packed up eight kilograms of his nicest beans and sent them off to the HCP. He endured the agonizing wait while the chocolate got made, the double-blind samples shipped to the tasting panel, the results compiled, and the genome sequenced at the USDA's Beltsville, Maryland, lab. Finally, he heard back: Congratulations! Your cacao is going to be the HCP Designee number 11.

The big announcement was made in San Francisco at the annual meeting of the Fine Chocolate Industry Association. Jacob flew up for the ceremony. There were 250 people in the audience, mostly pros. The emcee was Ed Seguine, an industry legend. "And he's talking about my chocolate!" Jacob says. "He's talking about pure Criollo, the only sample they've ever seen, the tasting panel has never tasted anything quite this, blah-blah-blah."

Tasting samples were distributed to everyone in the audience, and Seguine led them through the tasting, extolling the lack of bitterness and the creamy caramel notes. "And I've got my little bar," says Jacob, "and I'm like, 'Wow! This is really good!' And then that part of the program is over. And basically, I get attacked. I get swarmed by people from the audience with business cards. Some people are saying, 'God, it's the best chocolate I've ever had.' Some are like, 'Hey, I'd really like to get those beans from you. I'm a chocolate maker.' Some asked if I was looking for a business partner. And I'm like, 'Business? I don't know what you're talking about. I just submitted a little bag of beans!'"

But he figured it out pretty fast. Jacob's three hundred trees had tested out as 100 percent ancient Criollo, one of the only examples in existence. The only others were a handful of trees that had been found by scientists in jungles in Mexico and Belize, which didn't produce enough beans to actually make chocolate. This was the first time most of these dyed-in-the-wool chocolate people had ever tasted pure Criollo, and they loved it.

The wheels were already turning in Jacob's head as his plane left the ground at SFO. A delicious cacao like no other, back from the dead, and it could thrive only in deep shade? That could be a flagship of rainforest restoration. His plan quickly came together: once he got back to Belize, he would plant a whole new forest of baby Criollo.

The Heirloom Cacao Preservation Fund has gone on to certify seventeen heirloom designees, with more in the pipeline. It's been an essential shot in the arm for the movement, raising the profile of craft cacao, improving our understanding of the connection between genetics and flavor, and bringing much-needed recognition to the farmers.

But it's no panacea. While it can help farmers find passionate chocolate makers happy to pay a premium for exceptional cacao, that's just one of the many factors buffeting cacao farmers in an increasingly volatile part of the world. And it hasn't been enough to ensure their livelihoods. Ironically, it couldn't even save its first designee, Volker Lehmann. By 2014, the year he was feted by the HCP, Volker was in the midst of a high-wire act in Bolivia. And it was about to come crashing down.

15

The Law of the Jungle

Beni, Bolivia, 2014

After our venture on the Mamoré River paid off in 2010, Volker Lehmann decided he was all in. Aurelio and Angel and his other contacts on the river were confident that they could deliver tens of tons of wild cacao every year, and Volker knew he had to move fast to lock up the supply before his competitors got wind of it.

But it wouldn't be easy. As we'd discovered, the distances and conditions involved raised the difficulty level in every aspect. The way to overcome that was to build a big operation. He needed a serious fermentation and drying center on the Mamoré, he needed boats and warehouses, and he needed to pay everyone involved.

So he made the rounds to funders, hat in hand, and wrote grant proposals. He had all the right cards to play—sustainability, economic independence, empowerment of Indigenous communities—and eventually he scored big. The Dutch government was willing to put up half a million dollars in matching funds. Volker just needed to come up with the other half.

Somehow he did, cobbling together a group of Bolivian lenders. It was a tough group, and the terms were not especially favorable, but how do you say no to all that money? Anyway, it was all going to go brilliantly.

When he talks about it now, Volker admits he was never entirely comfortable with the situation. For a good old-fashioned control freak, there were always too many variables, too many factors out of his hands. "There's a certain limit to what you can handle at a distance," he says. "And when you lose control more and more, things can get really bad."

But year one, they were really good. He hired a crew, and they built a beautiful facility high upriver. From there, people up and down the Mamoré could drop off wet beans they'd collected, and boats could be sent to settlements like Combate for regular pickups. The fermentation would be top-notch. Transport to Trinidad aboard *Sundance* would be predictable and safe. Wild Beniano cacao would take the world by storm.

That first year, he produced more cacao than ever. Not quite as much as he'd projected, but it was enough to make his loan payments and to continue to build out his operation. The quality was awesome. Felchlin was happy. His Bolivian lenders were happy. The Dutch were happy. The people on the Mamoré were happy. And Volker was very, very happy. He felt like the system he'd always envisioned in his mind was finally firing on all cylinders. Just a few more years of bumper crops, and everything would be under control.

Then came year two. The cacao season got off to an unusually slow start. Volker eyed the volumes coming down to

Trinidad and felt the first quivers of discomfort. But when he quizzed his upriver team, they said everything was normal. "I was on very good terms with them, so I trusted them," he says. "And I asked, 'Will there be cacao?' And they said, 'Yeah, yeah, there will be a lot of cacao. But we need money for food and gas and camping equipment.'"

That, of course, was in addition to all the money he had to send with his team to buy the actual cacao from the pickers. It all added up to a lot more money than expected, because with harvests down in the more accessible spots, they were going to have to go a lot deeper into the jungle to find people with cacao. Just like the old harvesting tradition, he had to prepay for everything, with the understanding that he'd get paid back in beans.

So Volker sent his team all over the Mamoré region with $50,000 to buy cacao, expecting to get $150,000 of beans out of it. Week after week, he kept waiting for it to arrive. "Cash flow is the biggest problem," he says. "It's a lot of money, and a long time to have it out there. And when boats and engines start breaking down, all of a sudden you end up with no cash on hand. Then things start getting ugly."

By the end of the season, Volker saw just how ugly things could get. Only a trickle of cacao had come back. No problem, Volker told his team. Just give me back the extra money that was for buying the cacao.

But there was no money. Somehow it had all been spent on the search. Even then, Volker didn't freak out. "I said, 'That's not a problem. Okay. You owe me for next year. We'll even it out. It's not a big deal.' And then I told my lenders, 'Okay, this year I present a loss.'"

But the lenders were not nearly as enthusiastic about revisiting the terms. "They said, 'Uh, what is a loss? Please explain.'

And I said, 'A loss is when you don't have earnings. When you're on the negative side.' And they said, 'Negative is no good. You have to give us the money back.' I said, 'The money is with the people in the jungle. I can explain it again if you want. I gave them the money, the harvest was low, so now we have to recover. And you have to give me more money so I can recover the loss.' They said, 'No. You have to give us the money back.' I said, 'I have no money.' They said, 'Okay, then we seize your assets.' So I ended up in a lawsuit."

In Bolivia, debtors have little protection. Volker's lenders killed his company, closed his bank account, and seized his house. They even put liens on Tranquilidad. Volker tried to convince them to take a long-term view. "If you do a joint venture, that's called risk sharing. Gains are split. Losses are split. Companies that have a loss take a new credit to then recover the loss. This is how it goes. You reschedule your debt. You don't kill a business where you've invested hundreds of thousands of dollars over a fifty-thousand-dollar loss. You would never do this. But in Bolivia? Yes."

His life quickly fell apart. "The sky was falling on my head," he says. "Everything went upside down from one moment to the next. I thought I was doing the good things, and all of a sudden I was in turmoil."

The business collapse was the final blow for his marriage, too. He shakes his head as the memories come back. "The look on the face of my wife, saying, 'What do you mean there's no money? There was always money!' Yeah. But now there's no more money."

For a while, surveying the wreckage of his life, he was furious with the world. "I had a stretch of rage. Pure rage. You know, with a gun in my hand, I might have killed some people." Fortunately, he didn't. In fact, he let it all go. Just when it felt like it might consume him, the rage evaporated, along with the striving, and he found himself strangely at peace with it all. He can actually joke about it now. "Buddha has nothing on me. I'm as calm as the river Siddhartha was sitting beside."

But he just wasn't up for the fight anymore. He needed a clean break, so he decided to just walk away. From Tranquilidad, from Bolivia, from cacao, from everything. To pay his debts, he took a job as an agroforestry consultant with Conservation International in Costa Rica.

The personal catastrophe couldn't have been more complete. But although he couldn't see it at the time, the greater mission was still progressing. The NGOs had come and gone as soon as their five-year grants fizzled out, but now lots of companies were working with wild Beniano cacao, using the in-the-field fermentation techniques he'd pioneered. There was even talk of the government permanently protecting the chocolatales.

Even more important, wild cacao was now on the radar of the specialty chocolate industry. No more skepticism about its existence. No more doubts over strange bean sizes. The new generation of bean-to-bar chocolate makers was primed to embrace new cacaos from new places, the weird and wonderful, to experiment and discover, to cut out the international corporations and forge direct relationships with the people involved.

It was 2014. And even as Volker was walking away from the Amazon, a young Brazilian woman was walking in. And instead of the soul of an engineer, she had the soul of a poet. And that would change everything.

Making Chocolate

For most of its four-thousand-year history, making chocolate was a pretty straightforward affair. Toast dried cacao beans on a comal, or griddle; peel off the thin shells by hand; crush the seeds into a black, oily paste; and mix that paste with water to make a stimulating drink.

Since that paste was about 50 percent cocoa butter, solid at room temperature, it could be formed by hand into mud pies, more or less, and cooled into easily transportable discs—stimulation on the go! When you were ready for a fix, you just melted some in hot water. The discs were rarely eaten in solid form. Cacao ground by hand is gritty and not especially pleasant to chew.

Once Europeans learned the art of chocolate from Meso-americans and copied it, they swapped clay pottery for fine china and added sugar. (A practice the Mesoamericans soon adopted as well.) It remained a drink until the 1800s, when industrial mills and presses gave birth to modern eating choco-late. These machines made it possible to efficiently separate cacao solids from cacao fat, then recombine them in different ratios, sometimes with other cheaper oils that made the heated mass more pliable, so it could be poured into molds or used to coat other confections. In the same era, steel mills came along that were capable of grinding cacao and sugar—both coming from industrial plantations in larger quantities and at lower prices than ever before—into microscopic particles, launching the modern era of grit-free, silky, affordable chocolate.

By the beginning of the twentieth century, the modern process for making chocolate was pretty much in place. For the fine chocolate this book focuses on, it now goes like this. Cacao beans are roasted, then cracked and winnowed by machine to remove the husks. Then the beans and sugar are ground together and refined until smooth in either a melangeur— a metal trough with heavy granite roller stones used by small-scale operations—or a steel mill.

Traditionally, the next step would be conching—slapping the liquid mass around in another trough with mechanical paddles for hours or up to several days. That process drives off some of the sharper, acidic molecules in the chocolate and causes other chemical reactions to take place through oxidation, resulting in a smoother, richer flavor. Conching used to be de rigueur for high-end chocolate makers, who were often forced to work with subpar beans, but it has been called into question by the new generation, who prefer superb single-origin cacaos and preserving as much of their unique flavors as possible. These chocolates often have fewer of the deep, fudgy notes characteristic of old-school chocolate and more bright, fruity notes.

The last step in chocolate making is tempering. As it cools, chocolate (like other liquids) naturally crystallizes, forming a number of different crystal structures. Most of these crystals weaken the integrity of the chocolate, leading to a cakey mouth-feel, a tendency to crumble rather than snap, a lower melting point, and those unsightly white "blooms" (which are actually just cocoa butter) you sometimes see on the surface of chocolate. But one type known as a beta crystal creates a rigid microstructure through the chocolate, resulting in a glossy finish, a snappy texture, and a resistance to melting. Tempering is simply a process of raising and lowering the temperature of the chocolate at a controlled rate, which destroys all the crystal types except for the good ones. Unless you've been hanging out in some rustic corners of Latin America, all the chocolate you've encountered has been tempered.

16

The Cradle

Amazonas, Brazil, 2022

C ruzeiro do Sul is a run-down river town on the banks of Brazil's Juruá River, in the state of Amazonas, the heart of Amazonia. Piles of strange fruits and fish in the marketplace, a waterfront jammed with two-story wooden riverboats jostling together, grumbling thunderheads, the scent of diesel and rot, rakish characters selling SIM cards on the streets. On the hills overlooking the river are the crumbling mansions of rubber barons from the first Amazonian rubber boom a century ago. I buy a blowpipe in the market, along with a little bottle of snuff made from jungle herbs. The pipe is V-shaped so that you can shoot it up your own nose, which strikes me as a brilliant innovation, though I'm not going to try until I'm back in the safety of a more familiar environment.

I'm here with Luisa Abram, a young Brazilian chocolate maker who has devoted her life to wild cacao. Forget bean-to-bar. Luisa is tree-to-bar. She makes five different single-origin chocolates from five different wild cacao populations on five different Amazonian river systems, working with the local river dwellers—or ribeirinhos, as they are known in Brazil—in each location. And we're about to head down the Juruá to try to save her masterpiece, a cacao with a ridiculously floral fragrance that has garnered a cult following since she introduced its product in 2018, but also a cacao that will disappear unless we can get the local ribeirinhos excited about working with her.

Luisa's team includes her dad, Andre, a banker who clearly prefers exploring to being in the office; her brother-in-law Fabio, a videographer who is documenting the trip; and Alef, a young local she has hired to run her cacao operation on the Juruá. Alef lined up our craft for the trip, a long aluminum shiv of a river-boat with pew-like metal seats and a torn tarp for shade, helmed by a barefooted river pilot named Ricardo, who now threads his way past the other boats and pulls up beside a floating wooden landing reached from shore by a rickety gangplank. We throw our packs, hammocks, and chocolate samples into the middle seats and everyone piles on board. We each get our own row. As always, rain threatens.

We started the day at four A.M. in São Paulo, home to both Luisa and her chocolate factory. Unlike the other people I've profiled so far, she actually *has* a chocolate factory, and that completely changes the dynamic of what she needs and what she can accomplish. But I'm getting ahead of myself.

From São Paulo, we flew to Rio Branco, a midsize Amazon city, from where we caught one of the twice-weekly flights to the tiny but spotless and hypermodern Cruzeiro do Sul airport, clearly the recent beneficiary of some government boondoggle, which opened for our arrival and shut again moments later while we were still standing on the sidewalk.

From Cruzeiro, it's four hours downstream to a settlement called Rebojo, which is a fancy name for a cluster of huts belonging to three families. It's the crux of Luisa's plan to make Juruá chocolate the most celebrated on earth.

Through Alef, she had sent money in advance to pay for a new fermentation station—basically, an open-air shed. She also sent word that she'd pay well for any pods harvested, and that she'd teach everyone how to ferment and dry the beans. We're hoping the thing got built, and hoping a few people show up for the weeklong workshop, and especially hoping that they have an extra cabin for us to hang our hammocks when we arrive. "Just a roof," I implore. "A roof would be nice." Alef says it'll all be fine, they agreed to everything, but communication is impossible out here, so he admits his information is eight days old.

"You never know in the Amazon," Luisa says, pushing her glasses up her nose and smiling fatalistically. "The next problem. The next adventure." She's in her standard road outfit of leggings, floral-print blouse, and rubber boots, her wavy dark hair pulled back in a bun. She's been making these trips for eight years, but this one's different. She had to leave her one-year-old daughter, Elena, back in São Paulo with her husband—the first time she's left Elena for more than a day.

And to top it off, she's twelve weeks pregnant with kid number two. The morning sickness, she says, comes and goes. But it's essential that she come here and show face. We need to convince the ribeirinhos that being a part of this whole crazy project is worth their time. If we can't do that, then one of the great chocolates on earth will be discontinued.

The town gives way to jungle, and there we are, the Upper Amazon, the cradle of cacao. In this corner where Brazil meets Peru, Ecuador, and Colombia, *Theobroma cacao* evolved and fanned out, forming a distinct family in each isolated river valley. The USDA identified ten in its landmark 2008 report, but everyone knows there are more lost families to be discovered. Bolivia's Beniano cacao made eleven, and we are heading for number twelve, which may be the most delicious of all.

The river is churning, swollen, barreling blindly along like some sort of mindless Lovecraftian god. Ricardo stands in the back of the boat, steering the outboard with one foot while scanning the surface for trees and root balls swirling in the current. We slalom the debris, punching through spinning mats of water lilies that have broken free. The flooded reeds on the banks vibrate with the force of the river. Luisa checks her watch. "We're on schedule. That's good. Otherwise we'd be arriving in the pitch-dark."

She's done that before on these Upper Amazon rivers, and she hopes to never do it again. They're mined with massive tree trunks, one end buried in the riverbed and the other pointing up like a pike, waiting to spear a passing boat and spill its contents. It's not a big risk during flood season, when the rivers are high, but a few years ago Luisa was traveling during the dry season in a motorized canoe that had to dodge trunks all the way. Even worse, the boat kept running aground. "We got stuck in the sand multiple times," she says. "And every time, everyone fell forward. Then we'd have to hop off the bow and push the boat backward." They ran out of daylight while still on the river, which made it even more of a minefield. Now she tries to travel only by day.

So I'm actually grateful for the swollen river, as it means we won't get piked, but I do have another concern that might seem petty were it not for the tone in the old explorers' journals I've been reading. Dealing daily with everything from heat and disease to Indigenous attacks, they saved some of their worst angst for notorious gnats known as pium, which can reduce tough-as-nails adventurers to tears. "Between pium-flies all day and mosquitoes all night, rest is almost impossible," William Chandless wrote in a report to the Royal Geographical Society in 1866, "and one is driven to and fro as if between the gate of Hell and Acheron."

And on this, Luisa is not reassuring, confessing that even many Amazonians avoid this region because of the pium. "It's just going to be bad," she says. "When they bite you, they leave these little blood welts. And if you scratch them, you're done."

So I watch the jungle slide by as the river draws us inexorably into the Land of the Pium. Once a mile or so, we pass a hut or two on the high, sandy riverbanks, always built on stilts to accommodate flood season. There are millions of ribeirinhos in the Amazon, descendants of poor migrants from eastern Brazil who came to work the rubber booms of the late 1800s and early 1900s, tapping rubber trees for the latex sap. The rubber booms were followed by the inevitable rubber busts, but the ribeirinhos and their kids stayed, learning to live off the land by fishing and farming. Although they never legally owned their land, they became consummate river people, expert in boatbuilding and every other survival skill.

But even here, the modern world seeps in, in a slow trickle of gasoline and radios and plastic fishing nets. The irony is that to maintain their independent lifestyle, they now need cash, and cacao is one of their only options. Until recently, they'd barely heard of chocolate, much less connected it to the pods hanging in their gallery forests. Now, perhaps, they are ready to do something with their cacao.

"I'm hoping to see pods on the ground already waiting for us," Luisa explains to me. If Alef was able to entice enough people to actually go picking in the gallery forests yesterday, then there will be a pile of pods in Rebojo, and we can begin tomorrow by teaching people how to break open the pods, scoop out the beans, and start the fermentation.

"What would be a bad sign?" I ask.

"No cacao at all," she says. "No fermentation boxes. No drying station. That would be the worst, because we've come all the way from São Paolo."

I can't help flashing back to my journey down the Mamoré with Volker Lehmann. Those, too, were river people, hoping to use cacao as just enough of a cash crop to subsidize their life on the water. And it hadn't worked. The wild harvest was too finicky, the relationships too fragile, the territory too vast, the people ultimately not that invested in keeping the project alive. Why would this endeavor turn out any differently?

At sunset, we finally pull up to a crumbling mud bank where a cluster of people await us. We lash the boat to a tree that we hope will still be there tomorrow and scramble up the bank. Two wooden shacks are set back from the river's edge on stilts, simple holes cut for windows. Paradise.

Our host is a guy named Zé, which is short for Zédaica, which is also a nickname. His real first name is José, but half the kids in Amazonia are named José, so he and all the other Zés of his childhood were identified by their moms. *Which Zé is that? Oh, that's Zé da Ica.*

Zé's a handsome pirate type in his forties, scraggly black beard and mustache, soccer shorts and bare feet, ropy with sinew and muscle from a lifetime of fishing and hammering, almost as dexterous with his feet as his hands. Like most ribeirinhos, his parents came here from eastern Brazil to tap rubber trees and stayed, squatting on the river and surviving by fishing and farming cassava. Zé and his wife live in the right hut. Their son, Maicon, who's twenty, built the shack on the left for him and his new wife when they recently married, but for this week they are back in with the parents so that we can use their place.

We're sharing it with a handful of ribeirinhos who've come from farther upriver for the workshop, and three guys from SOS Amazônia, a nonprofit that works to improve the livelihoods of these far-flung communities. The organization was founded in the 1980s by activists allied with Chico Mendes, the rubber tapper who led the fight for the preservation of the Amazon and its traditional peoples. Mendes was murdered by a cattle rancher in 1988, but SOS Amazônia fights on, restoring deforested areas and teaching Amazonian communities ways to make a living off the standing forest. They used to focus mostly on rubber and wild palm oil, but thanks to Luisa, they have become cacao curious.

It was SOS Amazônia that first alerted Luisa to the cacao here on the Juruá, hoping she'd get involved, and they're here to learn how to do the fermentation so they can take that knowledge to even more distant communities. Luisa, they know, can't be everywhere, but maybe her techniques can.

The three guys are young, smart, born in Amazonia and familiar with its ways. That earns them a lot of street cred—or river cred, in this case. And that's the first difference I notice compared to the situation in Bolivia: a grassroots nonprofit deeply tied to the local communities and interested in partnering with a commercial chocolate maker.

And so far, the news is good. Awaiting us in the still-smells-like-sawdust fermentation shed in front of Zé's cabin are 4,200 pods, collected yesterday by a few dozen ribeirinhos up and down the Juruá. We've got a workshop.

But right now the pium are flaying our wrists and ankles and eyes, and as darkness falls, we've got a simple mission: get our hammocks hung in Maicon's cabin. We pull on headlamps and pound nails, hoping the thin walls of the cabin can hold all eleven of us—Luisa and ten guys. There's a quick meal of fried cassava, the staple for all Amazonia, and rainwater collected off the roof, and then we zip ourselves into our hammocks before the bugs can take any more flesh. It's a noisy night. Snoring. Downpours. And the distant hiss of the rising river clawing at its banks. The rainy season has just begun.

17

What Do You Do When Your Chocolate Sucks?

São Paulo and Acre, Brazil,
2014–17 and 2022

In the morning, we step out of our cabin and peer at the world: a strip of ground between the river and the jungle, planted with banana and cacao trees. Pigs and chickens wander under the huts, harassed by an old dog. The rain has let up, though the jungle is still dripping.

Andre Banks, Luisa's dad, is the first one up, and he can hardly wait to get started. He loves leaving São Paulo and coming out "to origin," as he calls it. He handles the geeky part of Luisa Abram Chocolate, poring over maps and genetic assessments from the USDA to figure out where the cacaos they are finding fit into the family portrait. He'll be collecting pods and leaves for the USDA on this trip, too.

We make instant coffee while the pium assemble in a cloud around our heads. Andre is over the moon about the 4,200 pods awaiting us in the shed. It's the best sign yet that the Juruá communities are interested. Now we have to hope that some of those families from up and down the river are going to come by to meet Luisa, learn how to work with cacao pods, and decide if they want to be a part of this crazy plan.

Soon Luisa joins us, looking like she got hit by a train. "First night's always the hardest," she mumbles. "After a couple of nights, you're just so tired that you sleep great."

While we drink our coffee and wait, Luisa explains to me that moonshots like this have been her life since 2014, when she decided to quit medical school and become a chef instead. "I had a boyfriend at the time who was in his fifth year of med school, and he was just so miserable," she says. In fact, everyone she knew in med school was miserable. No sleep, no normal family life, completely ground down. "I was just like, 'I don't want this life.'"

What kind of life did she want? When she tried to picture what would make her happy if she had to do it every single day, one option jumped out. "I love, love, love cooking! All my life, I've loved spending time in the kitchen with my grandma and my whole family. For me, food was always a comforting part of the day. So I was like, 'Okay, I'm going to culinary school!'"

That felt right to her. But she couldn't imagine breaking the news to her high-achieving family. Her dad has a Ph.D. in economics. Her mom works with software. Her sister is a lawyer. Doctor Luisa would have fit right in. Chef Luisa? Not so much. So she kept her thoughts to herself and took the culinary school entrance exam in secret. "It was perfect. If I didn't pass the exam, I didn't even have to tell them I applied."

But she did pass, of course, and then she broke the news to her parents, who were mortified. They tried to talk her out of it. But she held firm. "I said, it's only two years. If it's a mistake, I can change my path."

At first, it didn't feel like a mistake. She loved making something beautiful that made people happy, and the camaraderie was a breath of fresh air after the cutthroat world of med school. But she also interned in restaurants around São Paulo, working herself to the bone, and that part she didn't love. Once again, ridiculous hours and no normal family life, and once again, a subculture of people who were deeply miserable. After throwing up at the end of one particularly grueling twelve-hour shift, she began questioning whether restaurants were the place for her.

And then, on her birthday, her dad handed her a copy of Francisco Migoya's *The Elements of Dessert*. Migoya is one of the leaders of the modern gastronomy movement, and his book combined chemistry with pastry in a way that spoke to Luisa's soul. "That was my passion," she tells me. "The first recipe was how to make your own chocolate. And I was like, 'Whoa, chocolate doesn't come from a bar? It comes from a tree? It's a *fruit*?'"

From that moment, all she wanted to do was become the Willy Wonka of Brazil. When she learned that cacao was native to Brazil, it seemed even more right. At long last, destiny was reaching out to take her hand.

Luisa ordered a set of starter equipment and set up a micro factory in her parents' utility closet. But she soon hit a problem. Eastern Brazil has a large cacao industry, but the beans are notorious for their nasty, green-banana astringency. It's the cheap stuff that gets dumped into checkout-aisle candy bars. That wasn't the kind of chocolate Luisa was interested in making.

In early 2014, she tried to order some beans from Hacienda Limón, an Ecuadorian farm with some of the finest cacao in the world. Hacienda Limón had been the next Heirloom Cacao Project designee after Tranquilidad Estate, and it was just across the border from Brazil, so the logistics made sense.

But customs got in the way. In the 1990s, Brazil's coastal cacao industry, which at the time was the third largest in the world, had been destroyed by witch's broom, a notorious fungal killer of cacao that is native to the Amazon. The plague was both devastating and surprising. How could witch's broom appear on cacao farms 1,200 miles from its home? It turned out to be an act of bioterrorism. Somebody had transported infected branches from the Amazon and tied them to cacao trees on farms in eastern Brazil in an attempt to cripple the Brazilian industry, which was dominated by powerful capitalists. And it succeeded. Since then, Brazil had banned all imports of cacao in an effort to prevent other disease introductions.

But that left Luisa in a tough spot. There was no good domestic cacao to be had, and no access to imported cacao. Her chocolate-making dream looked hopeless.

But a few months later, a breakthrough arrived from an unexpected quarter. Luisa had an aunt who traveled through the rural parts of Amazonia, implementing new educational curricula in the public schools. She was working in Acre, a state in the heart of Amazonia, and she heard about a cooperative on the remote Purus River that was harvesting wild cacao. She didn't know any details, but she excitedly passed the info to Luisa.

Luisa was transfixed. *Wild* cacao? Straight out of the Amazon? She'd never heard of such a thing, but it stirred her soul. "I fell in love with the story," she says. "Crossing Brazil to go deep into the forest to get the wild cacao and then bringing it back to make chocolate—it was just so enchanting to me."

The co-op had no website or online presence, but after two weeks of phone calls, Luisa finally got the president on the phone. Her timing couldn't have been better. Since 2007, the cooperative had been harvesting wild cacao up and down the Purus River and selling it to a German chocolate company, but the German company had recently been acquired by a multinational that killed the deal. The co-op had no buyers, and was eager to find a new one . . . When was she coming?

Luisa was all of twenty-two at the time. "My dad was like, 'No way are you going alone. I'm going with you.'" So in August they flew into Rio Branco, where they managed to hit the cavalhada, an equestrian festival, in full swing. "It was so funny," Luisa says. "It was just a carnival of horses. Everyone drunk, everyone riding. I had no idea this existed in the twenty-first century." It took them hours to cut across town through the sea of horses and riders, then they picked up a dirt road and drove through the night to another town called Boca do Acre, where the Acre River meets the Purus. As morning rose, they met the co-op's president, hopped aboard a motorized canoe, and sped away into the jungle.

It was the dry season, and Luisa quickly realized what that meant. "The river was so dangerous. Oh my gosh! I've never seen so many trunks and obstacles." Just when Luisa and Andre were wondering what the hell they'd gotten themselves into, they turned off the Purus onto a small creek just wide enough for the boat. And followed it . . . forever. "I remember it was six hours in the little creek," Luisa says, "and then suddenly you see this big-ass bridge over the river."

They motored beneath the covered wooden bridge, between pilings made of huge tree trunks, and emerged into a hilly clearing filled with footpaths and houses and dominated by an open-sided wooden church shaped like a giant starfish.

Luisa immediately noticed one mysterious change. "Here we are in the Amazon, where everything wants to eat us alive. And suddenly, we get to this place and we don't hear a single mosquito. And I was like, 'Where am I?' And they're like, 'You're in heaven.'"

Céu do Mapía, to be precise. Heaven of Mapía. Luisa had stumbled into the heart of a psychedelic utopia.

Mapía, a town of six hundred people, was carved out of the jungle by devotees of Santo Daime, a religion based on ayahuasca, a drink brewed from psychoactive plants that triggers visions and euphoria. Santo Daime, the "holy gift," combines Catholicism with African and Amazonian nature religions. Its practitioners drink ayahuasca in group rituals that involve chanting and dancing all night long, everyone locked in a hallucinatory mind meld. They believe the ayahuasca—or Daime, as they call it—brings the spirit of the divine into them.

Luisa didn't know what to think. "I had no idea," she says. "What was ayahuasca? What was Daime? It was just so unexpected." For her banker dad, the ayahuasca cult was a huge red flag, but Luisa got a good vibe from the place. "I got a sense that they were good people," she says. "They were really conscious about the environment and preserving a good relationship with Mother Earth. And they were poor, but always in good spirits.

There was no bad coming from them. So I thought it was amazing."

Santo Daime was founded in Amazonia in the 1930s by a poor rubber tapper named Raimundo Irineu Serra, who was raised Catholic. Living in the jungle, he met Indigenous shamans, who shared ayahuasca with him. Under its influence, he looked up at the moon and saw the Virgin Mary, whom he called the Queen of the Forest.

At that moment, he became a spiritual missionary, incorporating the trappings of Catholicism into a psychedelic nature religion that spread among rubber tappers, pulling in poor souls from all corners of the Amazon. Although Daimistas' core beliefs were Christian, the rainforest was the natural vessel for their devotion, every tree imbued with the spirit of their goddess. Like the followers of many utopian movements before them, they developed an ethos of self-sufficiency, living off the land in simple harmony with their environment.

That veneration worked better when Acre was still filled with pristine jungle, but in the 1970s settlers from eastern Brazil began arriving en masse, clearing the forests for cattle ranching. The cities mushroomed. The Daime devotees saw the ruination of the land around them and decided to escape.

In 1983, the core Santo Daime members traveled for days, deep into the Amazon, looking for a new home. Eventually they landed at an old rubber camp on the banks of Mapía creek, a tributary of the Purus River. There, they were joined by hundreds of others, forming Céu do Mapía and living communally in dwellings built from local materials, raising their own food and throwing themselves into their weekly ayahuasca sacrament, with everyone from the children to the oldest members tripping until dawn.

But the Mapía community was never able to grow enough food or to be totally self-sufficient. They always needed things from mainstream society, so they always had a need for money. At first, they would tap rubber, just like in the old days. But in the 1990s, the rubber market collapsed. They had to come up with something else.

And that was when they turned to the wild cacao trees in the area. An NGO hooked them up with the German company, which was eager to support sustainable initiatives in the Amazon. The Germans gave them a crash course in fermentation and drying, helped them build a shed with some fermentation boxes, and paid a premium price.

And then the Germans got bought out and it all came to a hard stop. And then Luisa called. *Destiny.*

If Luisa really was to be the Daimistas' salvation, destiny had chosen a strange package for their delivery. "I arrived wearing fancy Nike and Adidas UV shirts," she says with an embarrassed laugh. "My luggage had wheels on it! I had no idea how privileged I was until I went there. Everyone assumed I was a tourist who didn't really care about them and wasn't coming back."

But they were wrong. It was everything she'd dreamed of. "I want to do something with purpose," she explains to me as we sit by the Juruá River. "I want to impact others' lives. I want to leave my mark on this earth." This seemed like her chance. Wild cacao, straight from the Amazon, produced by nature-loving people living in harmony with the forest. The fact that the community had been selling for years to a German chocolate maker also seemed like a good sign. "Europe has such a strong tradition in chocolate. I thought, 'If it's good enough for the Germans, it's good enough for me.'"

She and Andre loaded their bags with twenty kilos of dried cacao left over from the past season and schlepped it all back to São Paulo, Luisa trying to contain her glee. She was not only about to finally become a chocolate maker for real; she was going to be doing it with extremely rare beans. The day after they landed, she stepped into her utility-closet chocolate factory, cranked up her machines, and made her very first batch of wild Brazilian chocolate.

As soon as it came off the line, she broke off a square of pure Purus magic and placed it on her tongue. And, she says, "it was just horrible!"

She couldn't believe it. It tasted cheesy, funky, mushroomy, with hints of ammonia and compost. She was crushed and confused. "I was just so disappointed and frustrated. I thought it was going to taste amazing, like the gold of the forest, and it ended up being so crappy!"

She ran it by some others to make sure it wasn't just her taste buds misfiring. It wasn't. "I gave it to my colleagues to try. And they ended up mocking me. Like, 'You went all the way to the Amazon to get this piece of shit?'"

Naturally, Luisa assumed she was the problem. What did the Germans know that she didn't? "I thought I was transforming this amazing cacao into garbage. So I changed the roasting profile. I tried refining it for longer. I even changed the sugar I used. I changed everything! And nothing worked. Everything tasted awful."

For the next two years, Luisa kept buying beans from the Purus co-op, determined to figure out the problem. Even though she could never make the chocolate taste right, she still sold the bars around São Paulo. It was easy to get them into stores, based on the strength of the story of wild Brazilian cacao made by a young female chocolate maker, but no one reordered, and her reputation in the Brazilian chocolate world plunged. People asked her to bring chocolate to parties, just not the shitty wild chocolate. "It was becoming a thing, you know? The stinky chocolate of Luisa."

She began to doubt her abilities. Maybe she was just a terrible chocolate maker after all, screwing up these beautiful wild beans. She fell into a depression. Maybe she just needed to quit and head back to medical school. To stop being such a dreamer.

In desperation, she decided to try one last thing. She needed to run it by an expert, a real pro who could tell her exactly where those foul flavors were coming from. And she was pretty sure she knew the right palate for the job: Mark Christian, the wildly opinionated chocolate blogger. He'd already raved about Cru Sauvage, so he was familiar with what wild chocolate should be, or could be. And he'd been singing the praises of the Heirloom Cacao Preservation Fund, so clearly he had a soft spot for these quixotic attempts to preserve rare cacao. Maybe he'd be willing to help? She pushed her embarrassment aside and cold-wrote him, explaining her situation. Would he be willing to help?

He got right back to her. *Sure*, he wrote. *Send me some samples.*

Which she did. The day the samples reached New York, he wrote to her again. *We need to have a Skype call.*

She readily agreed. And when the date came, she poured herself a coffee, opened up her laptop, swallowed hard, and launched the Skype that changed her life.

18

The Queen of the Forest

Acre, Brazil, 2017

"C hocolate forms this sort of vortex," Mark Christian tells me, "and it sucks you in. And you keep getting deeper and deeper into it. And before you know it, it's a chocolate-covered world!"

Mark's life has been dipped in chocolate since 2010, when he launched the C-spot, his online "watering hole," as he calls it, for all things chocolate, which he unveiled at a special chocolate symposium at the Smithsonian Institution. The C-spot includes elaborate reviews of new bars, many written by Mark himself, along with surprisingly in-depth information on the science and history of chocolate.

Mark's introduction to craft chocolate had come by accident a few years earlier, as he'd been walking down Eighteenth Street in New York City past the Metro Pavilion. "I saw this line out the door, primarily women. And I asked, 'What are you guys doing?' And they said, 'We're going to the Chocolate Show!' And I was like, '*The Chocolate Show? Seriously?*'"

Mark's a serial entrepreneur. In the 1990s he ran a discount travel site. ("We got you across the ocean for a hundred bucks, but you had to fly standby.") That morphed into an events-management business. One of his clients was the Cannabis Cup in Amsterdam. And as soon as he slipped into the Chocolate Show and began walking around, he got déjà vu. "It was the same crowd," he says. "They were such a captive, passionate group, and the room was vibing almost the same."

Inside the Metro Pavilion, he bumped into Alessio Tessieri of Amedei Chocolate, who gave him a quick crash course in fine chocolate, including a tasting of Amedei's Chuao bar. Mark was sold. Not just on the glories of good chocolate, but on the business of it, too. From the buzz in the pavilion, he could tell the United States was about to get very serious about chocolate. And he wanted in. So he launched the C-spot and dove deep, training himself to be the first chocolate critic with an exhaustive knowledge of regions, varieties, and terroir.

His guide in this unlikely quest was an obscure 1944 book titled *The Genetic Diversity of Cacao and Its Utilization*. He blundered into it in a small bookstore on Upper Broadway and bartered some jazz LPs for it. (One of Mark's previous lives was in the music business. He has the liquid voice and cadence of a late-night jazz host, and the record collection to go with it.) Its author, Basil Bartley, had spent years traversing the Amazon and collecting samples, but he wasn't a writer, and his book was punishingly technical. Mark may have been the only person other than the author to finish it. "It was such a slog," he says. "I mean, seriously, actually hacking and whacking your way through the Amazon would have gone quicker than reading this book."

THE QUEEN OF THE FOREST

But he did finish, and by the time he had, his ideas about chocolate had turned on their head. Mark was convinced that every major watershed in the Amazon might hold its own uniquely magical cacao, and the idea that they might disappear before we ever got the chance to make them into chocolate felt like losing the ancient library of Alexandria all over again. "There are certain things that we preserve because they have value," Mark says. "And those good cacaos in Amazonia are the crown jewels, the rock stars of this global phenom called chocolate."

In addition to the gastronomical adventure of it, the quest to discover these cacaos might also help give people with no other connection to the Amazon a tangible reason for protecting it. "Forget acai or Brazil nuts or howler monkeys," Mark says. "Chocolate is the rainforest ambassador to humanity, because billions of people *love* it."

Mark devoted a lot of his work to helping people make those connections. He wrote about it on the C-spot. He guided the Heirloom Cacao Preservation Fund for a spell. He even launched an initiative called Landmark Wild Chocolate Reserve to spur the hunt for these lost jewels.

His efforts garnered some nice media attention, along with a wave of interest in heirloom cacao varieties that were already being farmed, but nothing new was being turned up in cacao's birthplace in the Upper Amazon, where he believed truly new families would be found, because nobody in their right mind was operating in such a remote environment. So when Mark received the email from Luisa Abram in 2017, he was intrigued.

Luisa sent him a couple of her Purus bars, made with beans from the Santo Daime community, and as soon as he tasted the chocolate, he nearly shouted with excitement. But not because it was good. "It was a qualified disaster," he tells me. "We don't need to get into the particular details of the flaws. They were manifold." Ammonia, manure, "a lot of other detritus with it. You were getting the basics, you know, cardboard, chalk, maybe even the blackboard itself. It was all there."

Mark didn't see that as a problem. Quite the opposite. "You can see through the bean, right? No matter how poorly they're prepped, whatever their postharvest technique is, the backbone of those seeds is still there. And what struck me about that cacao was that it could be good enough to be the ultimate dark milk chocolate, potentially without any dairy whatsoever. That's how much it was cream-puffing the oral chamber. It was great, but it was masked."

Translation: the Purus beans were being ruined by horrendous off-flavors, but behind those flaws he could detect some of the richest, roundest, creamiest chocolate he'd tasted. Most important of all, those particular off-flavors were extremely familiar to Mark. He'd traveled the globe tasting cacao, and he'd encountered ammonia and manure on four continents. Those were the classic flavors of terrible fermentation. And they were eminently fixable.

It's not you, Mark told Luisa over Skype, and it's not your beans, either. In fact, they're amazing. "I told her, there's something there, in that valley. Don't let it go! Let's get this right."

Mark connected Luisa with two men who would change the trajectory of her chocolate, and her life. One was Lyndel Meinhardt, who runs the USDA's cacao program. An expert on cacao genetics with a longtime interest in heirloom varieties, Lyndel was also married to a Brazilian woman, so he spent a lot of time in the country. On his next visit, he stopped by Luisa's factory with an assortment of single-origin chocolate samples.

"Lyndel opened the doors of chocolatey heaven for us," Luisa says with warmth. "That was the first time I tasted different origins. Same protocols, same percentage of cacao, all so different. Hawai'i, Madagascar, Costa Rica, Ecuador. I was just so amazed at how one could taste so fruity, and another kind of buttery, and another like fudge. It was just messing with my head! I'd been taking wine classes, which are all about terroir, and I was like, 'Wow, cacao has terroir! This is a whole new world!' And I thought, Okay, my chocolate really sucks in comparison to this, but if I fix the fermentation, maybe mine could be this good."

To do that, she turned to the second man Mark recommended, Dan O'Doherty, the Cacao Whisperer. Dan had been getting his master's degree in seaweed genetics at the University of Hawai'i before he noticed a cacao tree with purple pods in the courtyard of the biology department and fell down the rabbit hole. He switched majors, and within a few years he wound up consulting with cacao growers across the state, teaching himself the ins and outs of farming and fermentation through a lot of experiment and observation. He had to teach himself, he tells me when I reach him at his house in Maui, because "the lion's share of written information on cacao is bullshit."

Dan had stumbled into a niche, becoming one of the only freelance cacao consultants in the industry, and he soon found himself jetting around the world full-time to help cacao farmers improve their quality. "I love it," he says. "Traveling with a purpose leads you to places in the world that are not typically frequented by tourists. And you're often spending every day with people that have had a very different experience than you. Staying with them, eating with them. To me, that's a super appealing way to see the world."

So when Luisa reached out to him and explained her situation, he didn't need any arm-twisting. "I'd always wanted to go to the Amazon," he says. "Honestly, I tried not to let it out, but I'd have done it for the cost of travel, just to go."

But he didn't have to. SOS Amazônia had just launched a new program called Values of the Amazon, aimed at promoting wild-harvested crops, and the organization was beginning to realize the potential of wild cacao in the regions where it worked—but only if the beans were handled beautifully. Dan got the gig, and SOS Amazônia footed the bill. In 2017, Luisa and Andre joined a collection of Purus cacao harvesters, SOS Amazônia staff, and ribeirinhos from other cacao-rich regions to hear what Dan had to say.

Dan is a skinny guy in his thirties with thick, dark hair and two-day stubble. He looks like a grad student, rather than the world's authority on cacao fermentation, but as he surveyed the Purus beans at the Mapía cooperative, his expertise immediately commanded the scene. He couldn't help wincing as he looked at the beans, which were some of the worst he'd ever seen. "They looked like rabbit turds," he tells me. "Tiny and almost black. They tasted funky. You know, moldy, manure . . . not good." His suspicions growing, he asked the Mapía collectors and fermenters to walk him through their process. Sure enough, he knew exactly what they were doing wrong: everything. "I almost feel guilty for showing up and being like, 'Seriously, this is what you guys do?'" he says.

The cooperative was a trainwreck of bad practices. As with other fermented foods, from wine to cheese, the trick to high quality is to get the good microbes to take over before any bad microbes can get a foothold. And that wasn't happening with the Purus beans. The pods were being allowed to ripen too much on the trees. Some collectors would be traveling the river for four or five days, picking, leaving the pods in sacks along the riverbank, roasting in the sun, for collection on the return trip. Sometimes they were transporting pods in filthy, mold-encrusted sacks. By the time they got the pods to the fermentation center, half the beans were already rotting inside the pods.

And even once they got the beans into the fermentation boxes, the bad practices continued. Sometimes the piles got turned, sometimes they didn't. Drain holes were plugged, so beans were pickling in their own vinegar. And they were being allowed to ferment way too long, until they were more kimchi than chocolate.

After he understood the situation, Dan took a deep breath. "You know," he says, "you have to be gentle when you tell people what they've been doing all this time is wrong and we're gonna change pretty much every step. You gotta have some diplomacy." But the Daimistas did not welcome his suggestions. They were doing exactly what the Germans had told them to do years ago!

Dan still doesn't know if the German company gave them terrible advice or if something got misunderstood in translation, but at that 2017 workshop, he just said, Watch and smell. And he proceeded to do it all by hand over the next week, talking his way through every step. Short collection trips. Break open those pods and get those beans into the fermentation boxes as soon as possible. Clean your equipment. Turn the pile to introduce oxygen and prevent slime from forming. Check your drainage holes. Don't overferment. Dry thoroughly but not too fast. Smell everything. The alcohol stage. Then the vinegar stage. Then the chocolatey stage.

At the end of the week, the cooperative was in possession of a batch of beans that bore no resemblance to rabbit turds. And all resistance to changing the process evaporated. In fact, they were thrilled to not have to deal with slimy, stinky beans anymore. They admitted it had actually become hard to find anyone willing to get into the boxes and turn the cacao during its final stages. This new way saved them a few days of labor and a lot of misery.

As Mark Christian had anticipated, the chocolate made from the new cacao wasn't just non-stinky—it was amazing. "I mean, it had these straight-up dried blueberry notes," Dan says, still a bit in awe of the transformation. "I had people taste it, I didn't prime them with anything, and they were like, 'Oh my god! It tastes like you ground dried blueberries into it!' It had a nice caramel base, a lot of aroma, a lot of flavor, really some of the best chocolate that I've ever had."

Luisa concurs. "It was a game changer," she says. "When I first put that chocolate in my mouth, it was like a drug." And then the feelings came rushing in. Ever since she'd told her parents she was quitting medical school for culinary school, she'd sensed their disappointment. And then the chocolate had been so bad. She hadn't been able to shake the feeling that she was a loser in some people's eyes, maybe even her own. Now, at last, she was going to make something rare and beautiful.

The Purus chocolate transformed Luisa's reputation in Brazil. She took what Dan had taught and introduced it to three more river systems, working with the communities in each one to craft a unique chocolate from their beans.

By then, she'd also developed a deep friendship with the Mapía community, and she wanted to try to understand them and their forest on a more fundamental level. "I knew that I was going to keep on going there," she says. "So I said to one of the leaders in the community, 'Can I be a part of the ceremony tonight?' He was really surprised."

When they heard Luisa would be part of the ayahuasca ceremony that night, the whole community showed up to participate. "I'm not gonna lie," Luisa says. "I was a little bit afraid. Like, if I take this, is it gonna mess up my mind for my entire life?"

But she was committed. As evening fell, she joined them in the open-sided church, the sounds of birds and bugs from the surrounding forest filling the air. Lines of people paraded down the footpaths, the men in white suits, the women in white dresses with green sashes. The central table was filled with flowers and candles as the church leaders poured out the cups of Daime.

Everyone said the Lord's Prayer and then they formed two lines, one for men and one for women. Luisa joined the women's line. When she reached the central table, she received her cup of Daime and slammed it. It was thick and bitter, like a mud smoothie.

She joined the women on their side of the church and everyone began singing. Guitars and drums and maracas and flutes filled the air. "A rainha da floresta," they sang, swaying in unison, "cria tudo harmonizado . . . Toda cor e toda flor . . . dentro do jardim dourado." (The Queen of the Forest creates everything in harmony. Every color and every flower within this golden garden.)

After forty minutes, Luisa began to feel lighter, as if she were floating in place. The dancing became effortless, the songs flowing through her. She closed her eyes and heard the trilling of the tree frogs seeping into the church, their rhythmic *whoo-whoo* merging with the singers, thrumming in her mind. The sounds turned to colors, brushstrokes of purple and pink, neon green, the lightest blue. "Eu sou o plantador de tudo," they sang. "Eu planto paz e planto amor. Eu sou colhedor de tudo. Eu colho fruto e colho flor." (I am the planter of everything. I plant peace and I plant love. I am the harvester of everything. I harvest fruit and I harvest flowers.)

Hour after hour, the singing went on, hymn after hymn. There was a second shot of Daime, and then a third. Waves of color poured through Luisa's body, swirled around the church, flowed out into the night. The frogs sang. The people sang. The flutes sang. She lost track of where her body stopped and the next one started. The bodies became one. The night became one. The Daime rose within them, around them. The Queen of the Forest pulsed from the trees and the river and the animals and the people. Luisa sang and sang. And then the night began to turn to cream, and then the sky was the lightest blue, and then everyone was hugging and saying goodnight.

Afterward, Luisa lay in her hammock, still floating, not ready to sleep. She was twenty-five years old. She knew she'd reached a turning point. She'd finally been accepted into the community. Not just as someone to buy their cacao, but as one of them. They were all in it together, all part of the forest. Her ears were finally attuned to the Amazon. Now she had to give it voice.

19

A Powder Room of Flower Power

Amazonas, Brazil, 2018–22

By midmorning, everyone in our makeshift bunkhouse has risen and wolfed down a quick breakfast of rice and beans topped with farinha, the dried, crunchy cassava meal that is the parmesan cheese of the Amazon. We wash it down with more instant coffee as we hear the *tuk-tuk-tuk* of workshop participants arriving in their motorized canoes. The clouds burn off and it's a sunny, steamy day on the Juruá.

Soon half a dozen skinny boats are jostling together on the flooded riverbank, lashed to shrubby trees that look like they could give way at any moment, and twenty of us have gathered in the shed to admire the pile of golden-yellow pods, picked by these same ribeirinhos the day before. Everyone is stippled with patterns of red dots running up their necks and arms and legs.

It looks like ritual tattooing, but it's the pium, which are already settling in for a full day of munching.

Luisa greets everyone and starts with the basics. Luisa Abram Chocolate works only with wild cacao from the Brazilian Amazon, and this cacao along the Juruá is special, very delicious, but only if you treat it right. Get the beans and pulp out of the pods and into the fermentation boxes within a day of picking.

She whacks a pod with a short wooden stick. It breaks open with a satisfying pop, like a piñata, and she scoops the innards into the open-topped wooden cubes that have been constructed by Zé and Maicon in the middle of the fermentation shed. "Now look at the color of these beans," she says. "They're kind of pink. That's not the best." Luisa holds up the broken pod. "See how this is golden yellow? That's too ripe. We can still use it, but we'll have to ferment it a little differently."

Then she holds up a canary-yellow pod. "This is perfect. Now look at the seeds." *Pop*. She scoops out a handful of white seeds. Those go into a different box.

The three guys from SOS Amazônia are taking copious notes and peppering Luisa with questions. They need to take what she teaches here and reproduce it for extremely isolated communities on the Iaco and Macauã rivers. During a break, Wenderson Silva, an SOS Amazônia guy wearing long black sleeves and a balaclava to keep the pium at bay, shows me videos on his phone of their first trip to those communities the previous year. It was two days by boat, then eight hours by ATV along the muddiest rut imaginable, then another seven hours by foot. My jaw drops as I watch the footage. The guys claw their way up slopes on all fours, only to slide back in the mud. Their ATV spins in slop up to its eyeballs. One of them carrying a full backpack pitches off a pole bridge into a creek ten feet below.

Wenderson laughs at my expression. *Insane?* Yes, but he swears it's worth it. These communities are still trying to make a living off rubber tapping, and they are too remote to have other options . . . except cacao. So they are going for it, but only if Luisa is involved. They need the guaranteed buyer, and no one else has the wherewithal and the willingness to make it happen.

That model could be transformative for the Amazon, because SOS Amazônia keeps finding more stands of cacao in far-flung communities, and keeps asking Luisa to help them with it. "It's all coming for me!" she tells me with glee. "I'm going to be the queen of wild cacao!"

For Luisa, SOS offers entrée into the local communities she might not otherwise easily get as a Paulista from the big city. "SOS helps a lot of people in the Amazon," she says. "They're welcome everywhere they go. So it's good to be with them. They vouch for us." That level of grassroots buy-in may be the only way to make wild chocolate work in the long term.

SOS Amazônia had already been working with the people of the Juruá River when its representatives attended Dan O'Doherty's 2017 workshop on the Purus and explained that they had noticed wild cacao in some of the other communities where they worked. Maybe the Purus playbook could be re-created across the states of Acre and Amazonas? They suggested starting with Novo Horizonte, a community of boatbuilders on the banks of the Juruá River, about a hundred miles from the Peru border, that was down on its luck.

Dan was all in. "I really jumped at the opportunity," he tells me. "It was a blank slate! Cacao that had never been harvested and fermented before! You don't have to combat bad ideas that have already set in."

In 2018, Dan and Luisa and Andre flew to Cruzeiro do Sul and boated down the Juruá to Novo Horizonte. It was a tidy settlement of people who were really good with their hands. They carved stunning canoes out of local trees. They built sturdy boardwalks for getting from house to house in flood season. And they were open to working with the local cacao if it meant another source of income.

Two brothers loaded the team onto one of their boats and gave them a tour of cacao hot spots up and down the river. When Dan saw the pods, he was stunned. They were tiny, ridged, and red, unlike anything he'd seen before. "That was cool!" he says. "No wild cacao anywhere else has truly red pigmented pods like in Juruá. They might have a little bit of red streaking or blush, but never fully red pods."

Inside, the seeds were the tiniest they'd ever seen, even smaller than in the Purus region. That would make them a bit harder to work with, but it also hinted at just how different this population might be. To find out, they took samples and rushed them to the USDA researchers for genetic testing.

But the real proof, of course, would be in the pudding. Dan ran another workshop for the Novo Horizonte ribeirinhos, who embraced the new challenge with the same precision they devoted to boatbuilding. "Everything was collected fresh and delivered the same day and broken the next day," he says. It was one of those rare moments when everything goes right, when the Amazon seems to be almost suspiciously cooperative.

A week later, perfect beans came out of the drying racks, emanating an extraordinary perfume. Luisa wasn't sure the perfume would carry over into the chocolate, but it did. "I was just mesmerized! I'd never tasted any chocolate like it." No one had. And the USDA scientists confirmed it. "They were like, 'This is a new thing! You guys really found something!'" On a genetic plot, the Juruá beans didn't overlap with any of the other original eleven families of cacao. Juruá was off in its own galaxy. Number twelve.

Perhaps the only person more excited about this new discovery than Luisa was Mark Christian. "People used to think that Nacional was the floral cacao," he says. "But this Juruá is something else! It's a floral bouquet. It's a powder room of flower power!" For Mark, it confirmed his hopes that a whole new chapter in the story of chocolate was about to be opened. "Bring it on! Now we're finding things! This is what it's about! Rediscovery!"

One of the first to get his hands on the new bar was Matt Caputo, who isn't easily impressed. "You know," he says, "with all the samples that I get, I eat anywhere from a quarter pound to a half pound of chocolate a day. I have to evaluate bars from over four hundred chocolate companies every year. Even though there's a broad array of flavors in chocolate, you get kinda jaded."

But one taste of the Juruá chocolate and that skepticism melted. "Luisa's Juruá is just completely singular. There's nothing else that tastes like that. I was really struck by how floral it was. It had this note of perfume, like jasmine blossom, but also tropical fruit notes, and really beautiful herbals, like anise and sassafras. Just intoxicating. I knew there was something really special here, and we had to support this chocolate maker."

That support was going to be key to the success of the project. To make it worth the ribeirinhos' time to track down wild cacao trees in the gallery forests, Luisa offered five cents for every pod, which made Juruá one of the most expensive cacaos on the planet. To make ends meet, she needed to charge ten bucks a bar, but the craft chocolate revolution had not yet swept Brazil. People there were still used to paying a dollar for chocolate. Luisa needed the U.S. market.

She needed Matt. By 2018, his import company, A Priori, had become the top specialty chocolate importer in North America, supplying more than three thousand wholesale accounts. He featured Luisa's Juruá and Purus bars in his catalog and on his website and they flew out of the warehouse. Matt was thrilled. Luisa was thrilled. Andre was thrilled. The Juruá ribeirinhos were thrilled. Good times.

Then came 2019. Luisa had produced six hundred kilos of cacao from the Juruá in 2018, and now she was hoping to double that. The infrastructure was in place. The people were ready. But nature had other plans. The rains came, as they always did, but then they kept on coming. The water rose so high above the banks of the river that the entire forest was swamped, with the pods on the cacao trees underwater. Harvesting? Forget it. Survival was the only thing on everyone's agenda. It was a total washout.

Luisa was crushed. But she chalked it up to the nature of doing business with Nature, and waited to try again in 2020. But in early 2020, just as the harvest season was getting under way, Covid hit. The economy shut down, and specialty chocolate sales went through the floor. To make matters worse, the Juruá flooded again. Not as bad as in 2019, but bad enough that no one was interested in struggling through floodwaters in search of cacao, even for five cents a pod.

Carina Santiago grinding cacao on a metate in her home in Teotitlán del Valle, Oaxaca.

Carina Santiago and her frothy chocolate atole.

Cacao pods come in a dazzling variety of shapes, sizes, and colors.

Flowers and baby pods growing straight from the trunk of a cacao tree.

Father and son cacao farmers at Finca Cuatro Hermanos in Soconusco, Mexico.

Olga Cabrera making chocolate atole at Tierra del Sol,
her Oaxaca City restaurant.

Left: The Heirloom Cacao Preservation Fund's Alyssa D'Adamo tries out a
metate at the Museum of Chocolate in Mexico City.
Right: Cacao toasting for a Maya ceremony, Belize.

Ancient Maya drinking vessels and cacao god, Museo Popol Vuh,
Guatemala City.

Pottery unearthed at Hacienda Tranquilidad, Bolivia.

Sunset over the arroyo at Hacienda Tranquilidad, Bolivia.

Volker Lehmann counting his dried beans at Tranquilidad, Bolivia.

Gatherers arrive with a boatload of fresh pods, Rio Mamoré, Bolivia.

The author stirring beans in the fermentation center at Tranquilidad, Bolivia.

PHOTO BY VOLKER LEHMANN

The author with an ancient cacao tree at Tranquilidad, Bolivia.

Young worker opening pods at Tranquilidad, Bolivia.

Volker Lehmann arrives in the flooded settlement of Combate.

Cacao beans drying amidst the floods in Combate.

The author and friends, Rio Mamoré, Bolivia.

Bathing Amazonian-style, Rio Baures, Bolivia.

Emily Stone of Uncommon Cacao with a Belize cacao-farming family.

Jacob Marlin harvesting cacao at BFREE in Belize.

BFREE HQ.

Dusk on the Juruá River in Brazil's Upper Amazon as yet another storm rolls in.

The tiny settlement of Rebojo on an old oxbow on Brazil's Juruá River,
and the Amazon rainforest beyond.

Midday paddle on an oxbow of the Juruá River behind the settlement of Rebojo.

River dwellers cleaning cassava on the Juruá River.

Luisa Abram (left) teaching three river dwellers to break cacao pods during the training workshop.

The author breaking pods as part of the workshop.

Amazonian riverboat for Luisa Abram's Juruá mission.

Luisa visiting river dwellers in search of new recruits.

Luisa pays a visit to a ribeirinho household.

Luisa teaches Maicon how to dry cacao beans.

But losing their favorite beans was the least of it. The whole company was in trouble. Their restaurant sales collapsed. None of the cafés that sold their chocolate were open. They were struggling to pay their loans. To survive, they needed to cut every project that wasn't profitable. And that included Juruá.

In May 2020, Andre wrote Matt a long email explaining the company's predicament. With sadness, he announced there would be no more Juruá chocolate.

"My heart just sank," Matt says. "I felt like I got punched in the gut. It was my favorite bar." Beyond that, he'd come to treasure his role as champion of rare, amazing, hard-to-make foods, and he'd worked hard for this one. Yet the email staring him in the face said that it wasn't enough. "I just felt this complete deflation of my purpose in life," he says. "Like, what are we even doing here? Nothing! Our mission is to preserve food traditions, but no matter how hard we push, there's just too many pressures, and we're doomed to fail."

Matt and Andre began a long exchange about the situation. How bad was it? What were the risk factors? What would it take to keep the Juruá project alive? The bar had developed a cult following. It was becoming a great ambassador for the Amazon and its peoples. Matt feared that ending things now would kill momentum on both the supply and demand sides in a way that might be impossible to revive.

Eventually he and Andre got down to brass tacks. The only way to keep the Juruá harvesters motivated in their difficult circumstances would be to pay even more per pod and per kilo of fermented beans. They would need to build more fermentation and drying sheds along the river, to access more trees than just the ones within shot of Novo Horizonte. And they would have to pay someone to run the operation on the ground every day, rather than trying to do it from two thousand miles away in São Paulo without any direct communication.

Just like Volker Lehmann did in Bolivia, they needed to flush a bunch of cash into the jungle with no guarantee of return. This time, it was a much smaller and more focused operation than Volker's sprawling Bolivian cacao empire. Andre estimated that it would take about seven thousand dollars—money that a tiny Brazilian chocolate company just didn't have in the depths of Covid.

After his exchange with Andre, Matt couldn't let the idea go. He began entertaining the notion of entering into a deeper relationship with a supplier than he'd ever done before—a deeper relationship than any business school would recommend. "I just thought, What if we prepaid them for the next harvest now?" he says. "You know, we were in our own scary financial situation—Caputo's isn't that big of a company—but seven thousand dollars isn't that much in the scope of our history, and a dollar goes a lot further in the Upper Amazon than it does in the States. We could possibly keep this flame alive."

There were lots of good reasons not to do it. Between Covid and the annual floods, it could be years before he'd see the bars he'd prepaid for—if ever. And there were dozens of other good chocolate bars out there that could fill the slot in his catalog, no strings attached. "I definitely did some soul-searching," Matt says. "I talked to my wife, Yelena, about it. And thank goodness we're of the same mind. We're not doing this because of how much we want a yacht with a helicopter on it. We're doing it because we love what we do. We loved these people, we believed in their mission, and we had an opportunity. And if we didn't take it, then we don't practice what we preach. So once we fleshed it out, we felt like we absolutely had to do it."

Matt had no illusions about the greater impact of their decision. "What are we gonna do? We're just a deli in Salt Lake. It feels like we're tilting at windmills." He knew the industrial food system was rotten to the core, and keeping one wild chocolate bar alive wasn't going to change that. "I know that if we're going to make a big, broad change for the whole world, we need to affect the system en masse. But I want to have some tangible victories along the way."

Matt wrote Andre to say he'd front the seven thousand dollars. He'd pre-buy all the chocolate. "And Andre was like, 'What are you talking about? It'll take you years to get your chocolate!' He just kind of dismissed it."

But Matt kept at him. He even raised the stakes. He said: I want you to charge *me* more per bar. That's right, raise my price. And then pass that extra money to the people in Juruá. Make them super excited to make this chocolate. And I'm going to turn around and raise the price of the bar in turn. This is going to be a special thing, and people will be super excited to buy it and be a part of it.

Andre resisted hard. His Ph.D. in economics was screaming in discomfort. But Matt wore him down, and they agreed to give it a shot. "We almost gave up," Luisa tells me. "But then Matt was like, 'You can't! Juruá is just too special! Please don't give up!' The reason we kept on coming back was because of him."

Matt sent the money. And Luisa and Andre went to Novo Horizonte and offered the pickers eight cents per pod instead of five, making Juruá the Rolls-Royce of cacao. They shelled out thousands more in building costs.

And the boatbuilders came through. In 2021, despite ferocious floods, they managed to collect three hundred kilos of cacao and ferment it perfectly in their new shed. The quality was impeccable. In São Paulo, Luisa turned it into chocolate, pouring it into new molds and museum-quality packaging Matt had designed, then sent it off to Salt Lake.

Matt vividly remembers the moment it arrived. "I'm sitting in my office, same place where I got the email from Andre. And our marketing coordinator walks in and puts a package on my desk. And I look up, and she's got tears in her eyes. So I knew it wasn't just another sample. I was like, 'Is this it?' And she nods."

Matt tore open the box. "And I'm so nervous. And, oh my god, it's beautiful!" The packaging alone set it apart. The black-and-orange cardstock opened to a map of the Upper Amazon with the Juruá River cut out to reveal the gold foil beneath. A card insert read "Guardians of Wild Cacao . . . we can't let it disappear." The back of the package identified the bar as part of Caputo's Preservation Program. "Even the mold turned out great," says Matt. "You can see all the little artwork. But then the big thing: Does it taste good?"

There are a thousand ways for chocolate makers to mess up good cacao. They can overroast it. They can underroast it. They can refine it so long that all the nuances disappear. If they temper it wrong, blooms of white cocoa butter can appear on the surface, and it won't melt right. So there was no guarantee. "But I break it. I smell it. And wow, it's really pretty! I'm starting to get my hopes up. My fears are subsiding a little. And I pop it in my mouth. And it melts really smooth. No problems with the texture. And then the flavors open up, and everything that I've loved about Juruá in the past is there. Within ten seconds, I know this is the best chocolate Luisa has *ever* made. And it's such a great expression of why we did this."

As the flavors sunk in, Matt says he actually started to tear up, too. "We did something. You know? We helped to preserve this cacao. And I know that other like-minded people are going to appreciate this and join us in this fight. And the beautiful thing is that the weapons we use are sharing stories and tastes of things that we love."

So 2021 ended in a small but tangible victory for the wild chocolate movement. A great bar didn't die. But its preservation was anything but ensured. Those three hundred kilos of dried cacao in 2021 were a big improvement over the zero produced in 2019 and 2020, but only half what was made in 2018. And still no one was making any money off the darn thing. If Juruá was going to be able to run on its own energy, they'd have to do better in 2022. They'd have to expand to other settlements on the river beyond Novo Horizonte, and convince even more ribeirinhos who had never tasted chocolate that this was a worthy undertaking. Even more than a new system, they had to build a new chocolate culture.

20

The Mission

Amazonas, Brazil, 2022

Through the morning, we break pods. Thunk, thunk, thunk. At first glance, the mountain of 4,200 pods looked daunting, but we're a big team and we make short work of it. The pink beans go into one set of buckets. The whites into another. Any rotten beans get tossed. The husks, too, go into the woods, where the seething biology of the Amazon makes short work of them.

There's me and Luisa and Andre and Alef, plus the three guys from SOS Amazônia. There's Zé and Maicon, our hosts. There's four women from nearby settlements. And there's a young guy in cutoffs with short, curly hair and strapping musculature. Aires is a boatbuilder from Novo Horizonte, the original collection center on the Juruá. He and his brother spearhead the operation in Novo Horizonte, and he's come here to Rebojo as part of the charm offensive. SOS Amazônia actually brought Aires to Purus for Dan O'Doherty's original workshop back in 2017, and he's now regaling the Rebojo crew with tales of that overfermented cacao. "It was gross," he says, making a face as he breaks pods. "You could smell it from far away!" He scoops pulp out and tosses it in his bucket, then grabs another pod. "And then, in five days, it all changed." Dan's new system impressed him, and he began to think that maybe it did make sense for Novo Horizonte to get into cacao. "Especially because ours makes the best chocolate in the world. So we should do it."

In every cacao region I've visited, the producers tell me theirs makes the best chocolate, even though half of them have never tasted the chocolate. But Aires is an exception. He's tasted Purus chocolate and a few others, and he's actually snacking on Juruá right now. Luisa has brought a huge baggie full of all the broken seconds from the Juruá production line, and she's handing them out to all takers. I don't bother telling them that these shards melting in the heat are one of the most expensive chocolates on the planet; I just try to snag a few myself.

Luisa directs a lot of her teaching toward the four women. When I ask why, she says, "Because they pay more attention." Which is true. But there's more to it. The Amazon is not a progressive place. Gender roles are still firmly established. Men do income-producing work. Women cook and clean and raise kids. (Zé's and Maicon's wives, for instance, were nearly invisible during our visit, staying in the kitchen or washing clothes in the swamp behind the cabins.) Luisa feels cacao is something the women can make their own. "It's more equitable," she says. "Having the women collaborate is very important for us at Luisa Abram Chocolate, because we're mostly a woman-run company." Luisa's sister Andrea handles communications, and the vast majority of their employees are women.

But it's not just equity. For Juruá to have enough harvesters is going to depend on women, because the cacao harvest coincides with the fishing season, and that's a dealbreaker for a lot of the men. "I'm not going to let cacao mess with my fishing," Zé says. Fish is food for the ribeirinhos, but they also sell their catch in Cruzeiro do Sul.

When the buckets are full and the pods are gone, we carry two hip-high, open-top wooden boxes into the middle of the shed and fill them with the beans and pulp. The boxes have drainage holes drilled in the bottom for the juice, which Amazonian bees have already found.

It's really only a start. To make a single ton of dried cacao, we'll need forty thousand of these small pods. I begin to realize what an uphill task it is to build a new wild cacao origin from scratch. We're going to need a hell of a lot of buy-in.

We cover the boxes with banana leaves to keep the heat in and the bugs out, and we break for lunch. I take the opportunity to explore this new world. The part that's navigable by foot is limited and ever shrinking. The river keeps rising, carving chunks of the bank away. We know eventually it will swamp the compound, so there's some urgency to get the workshop done.

The woods behind the huts will also soon be underwater. The huts are built on the natural levee formed by years of flooding, but the land drops away on the other side into the most Dagoba-looking swamp I've ever seen. Trees with spiked trunks stand in the water. The still, brown surface swirls with slithery ripples. Giant Victoria water lilies dot the swamp, their six-foot round leaves looking for all the world like serving trays with raised edges. This is where we're supposed to bathe. Somebody has thrown a couple of rickety planks across a stump, and there's a metal bowl for scooping swamp water over your head. It's not clear that the whole experience would be a net gain in cleanliness.

But the forest is beautiful. I follow the high ground around the edge of the swamp through towering ceiba trees, their buttresses snaking across the floor like Andy Goldsworthy installations. I thread a path through skinny acai palms sprouting garlands of purple fruit fifty feet up. Tree frogs scooch out of my way.

Zé finds me back there and bangs on a tree trunk with a gleam in his eye. Giant black ants come boiling out, looking for the attacker. I know exactly what they are from my Bolivia misfortunes and I give Zé a pained expression. He snickers, then hops away on his bare feet.

To jump-start Juruá's cacao economy, we have two objectives. We need the collection points and fermentation centers—Rebojo plus Novo Horizonte—but we also need the collectors. And we need a lot of them. The chocolatales of Bolivia, with hundreds of cacao trees per acre, are an exception, but most wild cacao is spread through riverbank forests at low density, and Juruá is no different. To cover so much territory, we need people up and down the river who can check their local trees. And that's our afternoon mission: new recruits.

Luisa, Andre, Alef, the SOS Amazônia crew, and I hop in our skinny boat and head downriver making house calls, hoping Luisa can work her magic. Our first stop is a leaning shack set back in a muddy field a hundred yards from the river. There are lines of laundry hanging in the rain and chickens milling underneath the shack. A cluster of gorgeous kids lean in the open window to watch us approach.

Inside is spotless, with scuffed tropical hardwood floors that would be worth a fortune in the States. Aluminum cooking pots and bundled fishing nets hang from nails. A pika-pika outboard sits along one wall, its motor shrouded in a plastic trash bag.

Luisa introduces herself, the SOS guys say a few words, somebody hands out cups of rainwater from a roof catchment, the pium munch away, and the conversation begins. Mr. Barriga, as he's known—it means "belly," a nickname he seems to wear proudly—fishes a little and grows bananas, pineapples, and cassava, but his main income comes from collecting murumuru nuts.

You see murumuru palms all over the Amazon, anywhere that gets periodically flooded. The trees produce huge crops of hairy little nuts the size of tennis balls, and those nuts are filled with high-quality fat similar to coconut oil, but even better for cosmetic purposes. Many cosmetic companies depend on it, and many ribeirinhos make money by collecting tons of nuts from the forest floor.

But the work sucks. The trees are covered in eight-inch black spikes that skewer anything that passes. Over the years, as pieces of the tree peel off, the ground around them becomes a natural punji trap. It's impossible to collect the nuts without piercing yourself. The ribeirinhos were resigned to it—you make a few bucks a day, you become a human pincushion—but that made Luisa's offer pretty enticing, and Mr. Barriga doesn't hesitate. At eight cents a pod, he figures he can make twice as much a day collecting cacao, with less pain. When the fish are biting, he'll send his kids.

The next household is in, too. They're a big family, and they'd actually delivered three hundred pods to Rebojo the day before. Their reasoning is the same: no spikes! Luisa lies sprawled on the floor, chatting with the kids, and by the time we say our goodbyes and head for the boat, I can see a smile creeping onto her face. "Nice vibe," she says.

But it isn't all so nice. We also encounter a camp of illegal fishermen from the city. They make almost cartoonish villains, spitting veiled threats through full mouths, food flying from their faces. They are particularly unhappy to see me. I don't think about it much until a few months later, when a British journalist and an Amazonian Indigenous-rights activist are murdered by illegal fishermen on a nearby river.

By the time we get back to Rebojo that evening, this whole Juruá thing is starting to feel real. Pretty much every household is on board. At least for now.

Luisa checks the boxes. The beans are starting to ferment in the steamy Amazon air, but they're not as hot as she'd like. We have only five days before we have to head back to Cruzeiro do Sul to catch our flight to São Paulo, and if the fermentation hasn't finished, she won't be able to demonstrate the drying part. All the rain is actually keeping the temperature a notch below infernal, and that's slowing the fermentation.

Zé finds me and drags me to the river's edge, where he has a new horror to show me. Lying in his dugout is what looks like a tadpole the size of an alligator. It's a seven-foot electric eel he just pulled out of the swamp. Forget the anacondas and the crocodiles and the tucanderas, he says, *these* are the things to worry about. They hunt in packs, electrocuting their prey. He says he got shocked once before, but he managed not to fall in the water. If he had, that would have been it, because the eels like to slither on your chest and deliver another shock to finish you off. It happened to his aunt, he says. They just found her in the water.

I'm still processing this when Zé says that the eels also like acai fruit. They encircle the palm trunks standing in the water and zap them, sending a current up the trunk that knocks the fruit off. Then they slurp them up.

Zé also says that when the moon is full, a shining lady rises out of the river and pink river dolphins dance around her. I look at Zé funny, but he just widens his eyes and nods in slow certitude.

After dinner, a Rebojo teenager shinnies straight up a fifty-foot acai palm, machete jammed into the back of his shorts, and hacks off big garlands of purple fruit. We pound the acai into an earthy paste and eat it by the bowlful. An unmistakable, revitalizing rainforest energy surges through my body, and I'm hooked on raw acai for the rest of the trip. The Amazonians watch me lick my bowl clean and nod in approval and reassessment.

But even with the acai, Luisa excuses herself early. "It's been seven years since we've been coming to the Amazon," she confesses to me, "but it's never been so tough. Today I'm twelve weeks pregnant. And it's just morning sickness and I feel tired all the time. I can feel the energy draining out of my body. Hammocks are good, but I'd trade for a sofa, you know?"

As darkness falls, the pium finally relent, and I sit by the riverside, watching chunks of bank collapse into the brown wash. Huge bats cut the air overhead, unfazed.

The Gospel of Chocolate

Amazonas, Brazil, 2022

When we peel the banana leaves off the beans the next morning, the whole mass is fizzing softly. Luisa points out the foam on top and the tiny white dots in the corners. "Those are the yeast colonies," she says. "They're eating the pulp and making the gas." She has us all lean in for a sniff. "You can smell fresh fruity pulp but also yeast, like in bread. And a tiny, tiny bit of alcohol."

"How do you know when it's time to turn the beans?" asks Maicon, Zé's son.

"When they smell strongly of alcohol, they're ready," Luisa tells him. "Not today. Probably tomorrow."

"Are the flies a problem?" The mass is speckled with Amazonian fruit flies.

"They'll go away tomorrow when the alcohol kicks in."

"Why is the box of white beans foamier than the box of pink beans?"

"Great question!" Luisa says. "The whites have more pulp, so they're fermenting stronger. You can feel that they have more heat, too."

Maicon is twenty, a handsome guy with an earring and a stylish haircut. Andre and Luisa take note of his interest.

The rest of the day we continue our cacao outreach, spreading the gospel of chocolate from house to house while we wait for the fermentation to build steam. We get a few yeses, a few "thanks, but no thanks, I'd rather be fishing." All in all, Luisa and Andre are guardedly hopeful.

In the afternoon, Andre and I peel off for a little science work. We tromp through the wet jungle, plucking a leaf from each cacao tree we see and slipping it into a ziplock baggie with a white powdered silica gel that will suck every drop of moisture from the leaves, preserving them indefinitely. These all go to the scientists at the USDA, who are mapping the genetics of the world's cacao and are eager to get their hands on more Juruá samples. As we push our way through the vines, Andre winces and grabs the back of his neck. It turns red, but I barely have time to examine it before my shoulders light up on fire like I've walked through nettles. We never figure out which plant is responsible. Just another piece of the Amazon wanting very much to be left alone.

Day three, time for the first turn. The fresh smell is gone and the pile is churning with acetone and alcohol. The fruit flies are gone or anesthetized. Using a plastic dinner plate, Luisa slices a thin layer of beans from the top of the full box and distributes them to the bottom of an empty box beside it. "Don't dig a hole down through the middle," she explains. "Make sure to move all the layers. So top goes to bottom, bottom to top. Middle to edges, edges to middle."

It's a lot of commitment for a community used to selling fish and murumuru nuts immediately after harvest. I wonder if the ribeirinhos are starting to have their doubts. Zé isn't even around.

But Maicon is hanging on every word. "How hot should it be?" he asks.

Luisa slides her hand into the slippery pile and has Maicon do the same. "Warmer than your hand," she says.

"Why not just stir the beans?"

"They won't aerate evenly. And then the chocolate will taste astringent."

After the workshop, we quiz Maicon on his interest. He says absolutely, he wants to make this thing work.

Even if it overlaps with his fishing?

Maicon pauses, then unburdens himself. That's just it, he tells us. He loves to fish, loves life on the river, but you can't count on it anymore. Things are changing. The fish aren't like they used to be. They're smaller. And there aren't as many. The reason is no mystery. Some days, Maicon says, there are *a thousand boats* fishing on this river, all coming out of Cruzeiro.

In the past few years, the illicit fishing trade has infected these outlying parts of the Amazon, hybridizing with the drug trade in bizarre ways. Although Brazil has strict seasonal limits on fishing, locals working for organized drug cartels poach fish year-round in their small boats, often working at night, then sell to larger boats operated by the cartels, which smuggle the fish to wealthy markets in the cities of Brazil, Peru, and Colombia. Boats have been caught with cocaine and fish in the same shipment. A single large pirarucu, the most prized Amazonian fish, can sell for a thousand dollars. Waves of violence accompany the fishing, and with virtually no law enforcement in the remote region, there's no way to even slow it down.

All this hangs unspoken as Maicon looks around at the only place he's ever called home. "I know we can't survive by fishing anymore. If we're going to stay on this river, we need other income. That's why I'm interested. And I'm going to work hard to make that happen."

After the conversation, Andre seems pensive. "I didn't know they were having such problems with fishing," he says to me. "I think they're really counting on us. So the survival of our company is ever more important."

But it's not at all clear we're even going to make it to the finish line on this workshop. The next two days, the heavens unload sheets of rain, lashing the compound, with both the river and the swamp behind the shacks rising fast. We slog our way to the shed, and Luisa walks everyone through the next stage of the fermentation, turning the beans daily now. With all the sugars in the pulp converted to alcohol, the yeast runs out of food and bacteria take over, converting the alcohol to vinegar. Luisa teaches everyone to recognize the sharp smell as it hits your sinuses right between the eyes, and to feel the scorching-hot pile as the temperature spikes.

But she'd actually like it to be spiking a little bit more. The rain is still suppressing the temperature just enough that Luisa and Andre are worried the fermentation won't be complete before tomorrow, our last day. That would mean having to leave the Rebojo crew before Luisa can demonstrate the drying of the beans. Not a great way to start.

By our last night, everyone is exhausted, and the Amazon decides to really sock it to us. A deluge, all night long. The river licks at the top of the bank. The swamp is now a lake, lapping at the edge of our cabin. Sometime in the night, I hear the explosion of one of the huge trees in the compound tearing loose from its roots. For one queasy, endless second, I wait to learn if we'll be crushed. Then the world explodes with the sound of the tree crashing down . . . nearby. It feels like the Amazon has sent its warning sign. *Don't overstay your welcome.*

By morning, the river is such a beast that I'm wondering how we'll make it upriver. Luisa is, too. "I just hope the rain stops today, or we're not flying tomorrow." If we miss tomorrow's flight, the next one out of Cruzeiro isn't for three more days.

But it does stop. For how long, we don't know, so we scramble out to the shed to take stock. The temperature and humidity levels of the beans are perfect. Miraculously, they held their heat and cranked through to the end. Andre touches the thick sides of the boxes. "I think it was this tropical hardwood," he says. "It's a great insulator." In many places, they use plastic barrels to ferment their beans. "This is good to know."

Time for the last step. Beside the shed, Maicon and Zé have built a beautiful barcasa, a covered drying rack. It's a long, wide wooden deck on stilts, with a stubby roof on wooden rails that can be slid back as needed. It's the kind of thing that would have taken me months to build, but they knocked it out in a weekend.

We slide the roof back and scoop buckets of beans from the boxes onto the barcasa deck. Luisa hops up on the deck in bare feet and calls Maicon up with her. He's already barefoot. As the SOS guys take notes, she and Maicon spread the beans into a single layer until they cover the deck.

"The first three days are critical," she tells everyone. "You have to dry the beans from the inside out, so the moisture can escape. Don't think of it like frying something in a pan, where you're cooking the outside first. Think of it more like stewing, slow and steady." She points to the sliding roof on the barcasa. "This is going to be your friend, because the first few days you only want to give them two or three hours in the sun. Even when it's closed, the heat will slowly dry out the beans. But before you close it, you do this . . ."

Luisa starts scooching through the beans with her bare feet, like a forward moonwalk, plowing them into windrows as she goes, then making the turn at the end and doubling back in a continuous, snaking path until all the beans are heaped in rows. "This keeps the heat in the beans overnight. If they get too cool, mold will start to grow."

Maicon keeps peppering her with questions. "Do I have to make the ridges every time I close the barcasa?"

"Every time you do it for the night, yes. But not if you're just closing it for a rain shower."

"How many days until they are fully dry?"

"Ten to twelve, depending on rain."

Luisa asks Maicon if he thinks he's got it, and he says, yeah, all good, it's a lot of new information, but no problem. When I ask how many boxes he thinks he can do, he says maybe five. Andre tells him to set goals. One ton this year. Two tons next. Three after that. Try to get up to five tons someday. That would be a really nice production, enough to support everyone.

But that's two hundred thousand pods. To get to that level, Andre says, you're going to have to plan ahead. Scout the river. Find all the shorter trees that are easier to harvest. Clean up around them. Prune a little. Make the paths obvious. Get a huge crew.

Maicon nods. He looks confident. Cocky, even. But all I can think is, *Two hundred thousand pods? On this river?* Nature better be in a good mood.

Ricardo, our river pilot, says that if we want to make Cruzeiro by dark, it's now or never, so we grab our stuff and say our good-byes and scramble for the boat and gun the pika-pika upriver into the current. Luisa's feet are covered in dried, brown goop that looks like henna. She dips them in the river and washes them clean as we go.

The river is scary, churning in our faces and throwing whole trees at us, but Ricardo has done this a thousand times. He hugs the bank, where a microcurrent flows directly opposite the main channel, and he zips out of the way of tumbling root balls without a single collision. By nightfall, we are back on paved streets.

A few months later, the finished beans make it to Luisa's factory. Both Maicon and the Novo Horizonte guys have come through. The Juruá production jumps to 1,200 kilos from 300 kilos the year before and indeed it is, in the humble opinions of Luisa and Matt Caputo, the best chocolate she has ever made. As I sample the new bar in the depths of a blustery Vermont fall, amid the swirling leaves and woodsmoke, marveling at this tiny piece of the tropics on my tongue, I have to agree.

And to think that it almost didn't happen for lack of seven thousand dollars. That's the piece of it I can't get out of my mind. Matt had to charge fifteen dollars per bar to make the numbers work. In other words, for the price of an utterly forgettable bottle of wine, we get to make magic happen in the Amazon.

At its best, chocolate is an incredible collaboration between trees and harvesters and microbes and chocolate makers, a store of concentrated meaning and relation to be mainlined into our sensory experience, no ayahuasca required. How many other examples are out there, on the edge of oblivion, awaiting their champions?

My mind keeps going to southern Mexico and Central America, the old stomping grounds of Criollo. Over four thousand years of farming and rewilding, what had that most refined of cacaos become? How many unique variations on gobsmacking? And where were they all?

And as it turned out, I wasn't the only one asking these questions. And the timing was right. Within weeks, I was again shoving headlamps and field recorders into my backpack, squeezing in one last ski run, and kissing winter goodbye.

Heavy Metal

In December 2022, *Consumer Reports* published a study that gut-punched chocolate lovers worldwide. It tested twenty-eight different widely available bars of dark chocolate and found that twenty-three of them contained amounts of cadmium or lead that could be harmful if eaten on a daily basis. Five of the bars exceeded the safe threshold for both metals.

Panic ensued. Major media outlets rushed out "Is It Safe to Eat Chocolate?" stories. My inbox flooded with people asking me if they should change their daily habit.

And the answer is no—unless your daily habit puts you on the extreme end of chocomania. Here's why.

The standards used by *Consumer Reports* in its tests were those set by the state of California, and experts agree that those levels are extremely conservative. California's maximum allowable dose level for lead is 0.5 micrograms per day, and for cadmium is 4.1 micrograms per day. That's probably unrealistic. Cadmium, for example, is a naturally occurring element in the soil that is readily taken up by plants. All humans have been exposed to it throughout history, and we already eat about 5 micrograms per day, mostly in our grains and vegetables. So we are all over the "safe" limit already, and the more veggies we eat, the higher our exposure.

But it's not clear that there are any health problems associated with that level of exposure. Studies linking cadmium to health issues tended to focus on crops grown in truly toxic soil contaminated by the industrial production of plastics, nickel-cadmium batteries, and so on. So yeah, don't source your chocolate from the cacao growing on the grounds of the old battery plant.

In contrast to California, the European Union sets the bar for safe consumption of cadmium for a 130-pound person at 21 micrograms per day. By that standard, you'd need to consume an entire 100-gram dark chocolate bar per day to exceed it.

It's also not clear that cadmium in food makes it into your body. Certain minerals and antioxidants (which are abundant in chocolate) help prevent the body from absorbing metals. So a diet rich in fruits, vegetables, and seeds like cacao may be high in heavy metals, but they may pass right through. One nutritionist who pounds cocoa powder on a daily basis decided to test his blood and urine levels after reading several cadmium-scare stories. As he explained on a post for the website TheChocolateLife, they were completely normal, and well below the level that would be considered concerning.

So if you eat a normal amount of chocolate per day, there's no reason to worry about cadmium. Lead, on the other hand, is considered problematic at any level. The good news is that how it finds its way into cacao is completely different from how cadmium does, and you might actually be able to do something about it by changing the chocolate you choose.

Lead isn't found in cacao beans while they are growing in the pod. It's in the dust that settles on the beans and ground while they are being sun-dried. And that means it can be avoided. Lead levels in the air and dust are worst next to industrial sites and places with lots of passing vehicles—roads and cities. Unfortunately, that's where a lot of the world's cheap cacao is dried—on tarps directly on roads or plazas, or sometimes directly on the hard ground itself.

Fortunately, high-quality cacao grown in rainforest environments, such as all the cacao I focus on in this book, tends to have much less exposure to waste products from cars or industry. Just one more reason to choose it, as if taste weren't enough.

22

For the Birds

Belize and Guatemala, 2023

From the Robinson Crusoe compound of thatched-roof huts at BFREE, Jacob Marlin's 1,153-acre rainforest preserve in Belize's Maya Mountains, I follow the trail past the ranger barracks, the one-room chocolate factory, and the hickatee turtle sanctuary into a dark world of shaded forest. Giant ceiba trunks disappear upward through the middle canopy. Cohune palms arch their thirty-foot fronds across the trail like a *Jurassic Park* set. Snakes slither out of my path.

After half a mile, the trail suddenly opens onto an oasis: fifteen acres of former field, quickly transforming into cacao forest; twelve thousand baby cacao trees, which aren't going to be babies much longer. The two-year-old trees are already my height, and already heavy with pods—much faster than anyone expected. Some of the one-year-old trees are already blooming. Two scarlet macaws flap away at my presence, hacking in complaint as they go.

I'm once again reminded of how crazy fast things grow in the tropics. Flanking each cacao tree are two shade trees—native species like madre de cacao, whose very name indicates its ancient use as a nurturer of cacao seedlings. These twenty-four thousand shade trees tower above me, the height of twenty-year-old trees in New England. But in Belize, freed from such worries as winter, they grow nonstop. In a few short years, they will form a structured forest with multiple levels of canopy.

And what will live in that forest? That's the million-dollar question. Researchers from the University of Tennessee scurry through the grove ahead of me with cameras and notebooks, establishing a baseline of data so they'll be able to answer it.

Jacob Marlin's journey into cacao agroforestry started with that 2006 Cessna flight, when he realized there was no way to completely keep agriculture at bay. It was going to encroach on BFREE and every other preserve in the world. So he'd better find some form of agriculture that was less destructive.

And so he began making chocolate with the three hundred wild Criollo trees he'd found at BFREE. That went smashingly, but three hundred trees just don't make much chocolate. If this was really going to be a thing, Jacob tells me as we explore the grove, he needed to learn to cultivate the trees. "So I was like, 'Let's plant some cacao! Just for fun.' 'Cause that's what we do here. We experiment. We're an innovation center. We're always trying new things. So we collected some seeds from the wild and planted them. We just cut little trails and planted them right there in the forest."

That experiment went . . . okay. The trees grew, but slowly, on a wild forest schedule, not a human production schedule. But the more he learned about the wild Criollo and its habits, the more intrigued he became. "This stuff's weird," he says. "It's just weird.

The trees are different. They don't react to pruning the same way. Their harvest season is different. And they are definitely rainforest plants. Don't put them in the sun! Don't give them *any* sun. These trees do best in sixty to eighty-five percent shade. If you give them thirty percent or less, they die!"

That may sound like a major bug, but for Jacob, it was a feature. A tree that could produce a crop in the deep shade of the forest—that *required* rainforest over its head—well, that was the holy grail of sustainable agriculture.

That was the idea, anyway. For years, it was no more than that, an interesting tidbit he kept in the back of his mind. Then, in 2013, the idea got pushed forward by an unlikely catalyst two thousand miles away.

In 1983, a thirty-five-acre site on the Sudbury River in eastern Massachusetts was declared the Nyanza Chemical Waste Dump Superfund Site. For more than sixty years, a series of textile dye companies had been dumping toxic sludge and other discharges into a tributary of the river. After years of litigation with the government, the parties reached a $3.9 million settlement in 1998, with the funds earmarked to restore the natural resources injured by the discharges. The deal was that the money could be used to restore contaminated habitat at the site, or to restore or protect other habitat used by the river's wildlife.

And this is where things got surprisingly progressive. The wildlife affected by the spill included a number of songbirds, including vireos, thrushes, warblers, catbirds, and flycatchers. These birds are all migratory. They spend their summer breeding season in Massachusetts, but they winter in Central America. And their Central American habitat was disappearing much faster than their New England haunts. And somebody smart managed to convince the Nyanza trustees that they could do a lot more good for their birds in Central America than in Massachusetts.

But where? Well, by then, Jacob Marlin had been hosting researchers from the Smithsonian and other institutions for years. "We had an incredible data set," he says. "We had Ph.D.s putting teeny-tiny backpacks on birds with geolocators. So we were learning all kinds of things about where the birds are coming from."

A lot of them were coming from the northeastern United States. They were the right birds. The scientists involved with the Nyanza project asked Jacob if there was an opportunity to restore bird habitat in his part of Belize. Jacob suggested organic, shade-grown cacao, which would be a win for both the birds and the local villagers. "And after years and years and years and years of meetings and report writing and data collection, we got a small amount from the site."

In 2013, Jacob coordinated the planting of cacao on five 30-acre sites in Maya villages near BFREE that had been degraded by years of intensive farming of pineapples, bananas, and corn. The sites quickly turned into passable forest, and Jacob had his first glimmer that cacao could be more than a fun hobby.

Then came 2015, and all that love from the Heirloom Cacao Preservation Fund. Jacob's plan came together. He was going to grow a forest of ancient, shade-loving, premium wild cacao. And it was going to be a model for the world.

To get his farm up and running, Jacob knew he needed a great agronomist. Someone who really knew cacao but who wasn't wedded to the old ways of doing things. He got lucky. A mutual friend put him in touch with Erick Ac, just a few hours away in Guatemala. At the time, Erick was one of the few professionally trained agronomists who had been playing around with Criollo for years, and he was ready for a new challenge. Jacob lured him to BFREE as a consultant, and he wound up staying four years.

It wasn't straightforward. No one had tried to farm these trees in a thousand years. It was like saddling a wild horse. The trees didn't graft like normal trees. They didn't want to be pruned like normal trees. They didn't love sunlight. And they certainly didn't want to grow as densely as normal trees. But over time, Erick and Jacob came up with a system that worked. They established a nursery full of the next generation of seedlings and a clonal garden full of grafted saplings from the most interesting wild trees. The first trees went in the ground in November 2019. They tweaked the protocol for the next batch in 2020, and those trees quickly shot up past their predecessors. Thousands more went in the ground in 2021 and 2022. And I got to wander through the rising forest, snapping photos of purple pods, in 2023.

That same year, the forest now established, Erick returned home. Taking what he'd learned, he became the Johnny Appleseed of Guatemala, assuming the presidency of Guatemala's Cocoa Quality Promotion Committee and teaching the secrets of shade-rich Criollo far and wide. He even took to the wilds of Guatemala, with a grant from the Heirloom Cacao Preservation Fund, to see if, as in Belize, there were places so remote that they might still harbor ancient strains.

In the Maya community of Uaxactún, a low, hot, incredibly remote part of the Maya Biosphere Reserve near Tikal and the

Belize border, he hit pay dirt. About sixty years earlier, the father of a farmer named Don Chico Pop noticed two wild cacao trees in the forest, growing near some Maya ruins. For the rest of his life, he'd pick the pods as he passed and use the pulp and seeds at home. Don Chico was thirteen at the time, and ever since, he's been stewarding the trees. A few years ago, he began planting seeds from them. He and his family have now planted about 3,500, a companion orchard to Jacob Marlin's. Erick is now teaching the Uaxactún community how to graft, how to establish a nursery and clonal garden, and how to cultivate new orchards.

One thing Erick has found is that Criollo's reputation for being a poor producer is a myth, propagated by "experts" who had only worked with modern hybrids. "People say that Criollo trees are too low-yielding and susceptible to disease," he says, "but we've shown that they are equal or better producers." Just as with Jacob's trees in Belize, the trick is learning what they like. Each is going to require a different regimen of weeding, pruning, shade regulation, nutrition, and fermentation. "There's no fixed rule," he says. "You always have to experiment."

The gamble paid off. While a typical African cacao farm, growing in full sun, might get yields of 250 kilos per hectare, Erick's shade-grown Criollo routinely produces 1,000 kilos per hectare. And it gets snapped up by European chocolate makers at super premium prices. "The economic model is working really well," Erick says. With his guidance, many other Guatemalan cacao farmers are catching on.

The timing couldn't be better. In 2023, the Smithsonian launched its cacao-certification program, Bird Friendly. Chocolate bars made with cacao that meets the Smithsonian's standards for canopy cover and organic production now get the institute's Bird Friendly logo.

The program is based on the work of Smithsonian ecologist Ruth Bennett, who analyzed decades' worth of biodiversity data on cacao farms and came up with some extraordinary results. To no one's surprise, cacao grown with little shade provided poor bird habitat, but cacao grown in a relatively modest 30 to 40 percent shade supported as much density and diversity of birdlife as completely natural forest. For some types of birds, including migratory birds from North America, it was even better. "Rustic" cacao farms having more than 60 percent native canopy cover (like the chocolatales of Bolivia) had even greater richness and abundance.

Not all types of birds fared better in the cacao farms. Some preferred natural forest. So even high-shade cacao farms could never be a complete substitute for wild rainforest, and should never replace existing forest. But shade-rich cacao now looks like a brilliant way to transform degraded farmland to high-quality rainforest, for the birds and a lot of other wildlife.

And it can happen fast. In 2023, the Heirloom Cacao Preservation Fund designated its seventeenth heirloom cacao: Kampura Farms, in Izabal, Guatemala. Launched a dozen years ago to turn the tide on Guatemala's rampant deforestation and to provide a model of socially responsible agriculture, Kampura Farms has transformed more than two thousand acres of old cattle ranch into flourishing forest—more than five hundred thousand trees in all. Its cacao is planted under rosewood, mahogany, and madre de cacao.

To see the before-and-after photos is astonishing. From beaten wasteland to rolling hills of Central American jungle. *In twelve years.* More than one hundred varieties of cacao. Sustainable work for four neighboring villages. When I imagine the future of chocolate, I'd like to think it looks a lot like that.

23

The Secret Garden

Soconusco, Mexico, 2023

We are six people squeezed into a Ford F-350 Super Duty pickup truck, rolling down the shimmering streets of Soconusco, the last little corner of Mexico before it becomes Guatemala, searching for a blind guide. Our leader in this endeavor is a guy named Ajax, sitting in the middle up front.

Ajax Moreno is a renowned archaeological illustrator, a veteran of some of Mexico's greatest digs, and he looks the part. Mid-sixties, a Santa Claus beard and belly, Birkenstocks on his feet, a compass and break-apart reading glasses dangling from his neck. When I ask from the back seat if he's named for Ajax from *The Iliad*, he nods and cranes his neck to appraise me with new eyes. "Yes! The hero!"

Well, sort of. Ajax did indeed do a lot of the heavy lifting for the Greeks in the early days of the war while Achilles was simpering in his tent, and he did heroically help Odysseus to retrieve Achilles's body from the battlefield after he was killed.

But he wasn't a very eloquent guy, and when the Greeks were assigning credit for the body grab, Odysseus talked a much better game and got all the accolades. Ajax, feeling underappreciated, threw himself on his own sword.

This Ajax is also complicated. He's a bit of a celebrity at Soconusco's famed ruins, but he's also been banned from some of them for conducting unsanctioned tours and generally not playing by the bureaucratic rules. And he talks a very good game. So he probably should have been named Ulysses instead.

In any case, fortunately, we're not looking for tourist sites. We want to go somewhere no one knows about. The place where chocolate began. "I haven't been there in fifteen years," Ajax explains as we drive. "I can't remember how to find it. But I know somebody who can."

I'm sharing the back seat with Alejandro Zamorano and Alyssa D'Adamo. Alejandro is the founder of Revival Cacao, which tracks down rare sources of fine-flavor cacao in Mexico and exports them to Europe and the United States. "My goal is to revive Mexican cacao," he explained to me. "To bring it back to its former glory." An uphill battle, he admits. "Mexico is the closest origin to the United States. It's very historically rich. But it's totally overlooked. Even by Mexicans!"

Alyssa is a videographer working with the Heirloom Cacao Preservation Fund. We three are the team for the HCP's first Discovery Expedition. After years of passively certifying exceptional cacaos that were submitted, the HCP has decided to get proactive. Most of the great cacao varieties still in existence don't have champions like Volker Lehmann or Emily Stone who can pull together thirteen kilograms of perfectly fermented beans, package them up, and ship them to Guittard Chocolate in San Francisco for assessment. They're just straggling along in some forgotten field or forest. If you're going to find these standouts, so they can be preserved and cultivated before it's too late, you're going to need some cacao detectives. That's us.

But mostly it's Alejandro. As the boots on the ground, he's responsible for finding the leads we'll follow. And most of them lead right here to Soconusco, the epicenter of Mexican chocolate culture. Chocolate's great journey started here, four thousand years ago, with a people known as the Mokaya. Somewhere right around here lies an archaeological site called Paso de la Amada, which yielded some of the oldest artifacts of early Mesoamerican culture. Ajax was on that dig, illustrating, and he's basically a walking encyclopedia of Mesoamerican archaeology, so he's going to give us the full scoop on Paso de la Amada.

That is, if we can find it. But Ajax knows a local guy who was the chief of the excavation crew during the dig thirty years ago. That guy will remember.

So we drive around and ask questions of a lot of people on the street and finally we roll up to a tiny shack. The guy is ancient himself, and nearly blind. I watch him feeling his way around the shack and don't feel confident in our odds, but the guy feels his way to a metal kettle on the stove, takes a big swig of water straight out of the spout, and says, no problem. He's got this.

And then we are seven in the Ford F-350, the blind guide up front and one of our crew riding in the bed, driving past rows of mango trees and cornfields in the countryside. Our guide keeps stopping the truck and asking us to read the signs to him, then calling for turns here and backtracks there. I get increasingly dour about our chances, until suddenly he raises his arm and says, "Here."

Here? It's just another field, lines of cashew trees stretching into the distance, the dark furrows shimmering with heat on this

April day as the temperature and humidity both flirt with triple digits. Here?

But Ajax is already leaping out of the truck and heading into the field, exhorting us to follow him. We pile out and trudge through the hot dirt, a farmer on a tractor eyeing us with disinterest in the distance.

And then, at the height of the land, Ajax turns to face us. "To come to this place is a privilege!" he says. "Nobody knows about it anymore. Maybe twenty of us were here, working every day. I know what it means to stand here."

Ajax leans down and picks a handful of small stones out of the dirt. Or, no, they're not stones. They're chunks of pottery, and they're everywhere. He holds up a black piece with faint patterns. "This is Olmec," he says. "After the Mokaya. Maybe one hundred years before Christ." Then he holds up a chunk colored brick red and etched in elegant lines. "This is Barra ceramics from the Mokaya people. Maybe nineteen hundred years before Christ. First pottery in Mesoamerica. Very beautiful."

Then he scoops some shiny black glasslike shards from the soil. "Obsidian! For their blades. From El Chayal quarry in Guatemala." We ogle the sharp flakes for a moment before Ajax tilts his hand and dumps them unceremoniously with a shrug. "It is the worst obsidian."

Okay, so maybe their knives sucked, but their culture was fascinating. Ajax explains all. Here, four thousand years ago, one of the first great outposts of Mesoamerican civilization arose, and chocolate arose with it. They both appeared out of nowhere, sui generis, as if two parts of the same cultural awakening, and they would stay in lockstep for the next 3,500 years.

It wasn't until the 1970s that the potsherds turned up by farmers' plows clued archaeologists that something interesting was buried beneath. After lengthy negotiations, they struck a deal: they could excavate the area if they hired locals to do the work and returned it all to normal fields after they were done.

Excavations began in the 1990s and struck gold. They turned up the oldest ball court ever found, 250 feet long by 25 feet wide, complete with stone bleachers for the spectators. There was also a palatial meeting house, 85 feet long by 30 feet wide, oriented, like all the structures at Paso de la Amada, to face Tacaná, the twelve-thousand-foot volcano brooding on the border thirty miles away.

And there was chocolate. Neckless jars at the site tested positive for theobromine, the psychoactive chemical found in cacao. They'd been saturated with liquid chocolate, used for ritual purposes. Here on the well-watered and richly volcanic plains of the Pacific coast, the peoples of Soconusco were farming and drinking cacao four millennia ago, and they never stopped.

We know this because the Mexica considered Soconusco to possess the finest cacao in the world. They conquered it in the 1400s for that very reason. More than six hundred miles from the Mexica capital of Tenochtitlán, it was by far the most distant province of the empire, the only one not physically contiguous with the rest, and the winding route between the two was heavily guarded. The deal was that the province of Soconusco (or Xoconochco, as the Mexica called it) had to send two hundred cargas (about five million beans) to the Mexica capital every year, or there'd be trouble. When the Spanish took over, they kept the same deal: five million beans, every year.

For centuries, Soconusco remained Cacao Central. A Spanish survey of one Soconusco town in 1582 found that 83 percent of the households had cacao orchards, with an average of 343 trees per household.

And then it all fell apart.

$\emptyset$

"Mexican cacao is in big trouble," Alejandro says as we drive across Soconusco, chasing another lead. "It's disconnected from modern trends. It's isolated, slowly dying. People are abandoning their cacao farms. Cutting them down."

Although Mexico gave birth to chocolate and gifted it to the world, it lost its place in fine chocolate long ago. "It was a staple food," Alejandro laments. "It didn't matter if you were wealthy or poor. Everyone was drinking chocolate every day. But this is long gone." A country that once produced eighty thousand tons of cacao now grows just twenty thousand. Soconusco and other areas in the state of Chiapas account for maybe a third of that, with the state of Tabasco, on the Caribbean coast, responsible for the rest.

The decline in delicious varieties has been even more precipitous. In the twentieth century, government programs encouraged farmers to plant modern hybrid varieties with higher yields. "The big multinationals get subsidies to kick-start farms where you have monocultures, just one or two chosen varieties of cacao planted in rows in the sun," Alejandro explains, "whereas in Mexico, cacao was always grown in an agroforestry system. Basically a food forest."

As they became financially untenable, many classic Mexican cacaos disappeared from the market. But not all. The saving grace had nothing to do with economics. "People in southern

Mexico are emotionally attached to their cacao farms and to their heirloom varieties," says Alejandro. "Most of them don't farm cacao just to make money, but because it has been part of the family heritage for centuries. Maybe the grandfather or father was very emotionally attached to the farm, and it didn't matter what happened, they would still farm it and still protect it. And as cacao has been growing in Mexico for so many millennia, the genetic pockets are very rich. There's a huge diversity in a small area. But these are being replaced. People pass away, new generations come, and maybe they're not that interested. So we're at a critical point. But you can still find hidden gems. Here and there, there are pockets."

We've been driving along a giant concrete wall running along the roadside, and now we turn into a gate and ring for admission. With any luck, this walled garden hides one of those pockets.

From the street, it looks like any other old industrial site trying to keep you out. Crumbling brick walls topped with razor wire and splashed with graffiti. It feels run-down, unloved, maybe even abandoned—all legit possibilities here in Chiapas. Waves of emigration to the United States have left the region with plenty of abandoned sites. So I'm having trouble believing anything magical lurks within. But then the gates part, our truck rolls inside, and everything changes.

We pass row after row of Methuselah cacao trees, green mosses coating their gnarled limbs like fur. Pods of every conceivable color and shape hang from them, reds and purples and yellows, from almost round to long and pointy. No two are alike.

"It's like a museum," marvels Alejandro, craning his neck as another weird pod goes by.

We pull up to a nondescript concrete bungalow and are greeted by Pablo Mugüerza, a young guy in blue jeans and a blue T-shirt with jet-black hair and soulful eyes. "Welcome to La Rioja," he says with a sweet smile. "What's left of it."

He brings us into the little office, which is decorated with diplomas and awards from the 1930s and '40s honoring Finca la Rioja and Moisés Mugüerza, Pablo's great-grandfather. Moisés arrived in Soconusco from Rioja, Spain, in the early 1900s and fell in love with cacao farming. With the help of his son, Anselmo, he traveled throughout Tabasco, Chiapas, and Central America, collecting every interesting variety he could find and propagating it at the farm he named La Rioja, in memory of his homeland. He built it into a 750-acre estate that boasted the most extensive collection of cacao genetics of the time. He produced two or three hundred tons a year and sold it all to Mexico's largest chocolate maker. He made a little chocolate, too, importing cutting-edge equipment from the famed Lehmann company in Germany.

Somewhere around World War II, Moisés stopped collecting new samples, and the orchard froze in time. By the 1960s, he was ready to retire, and he divided the estate among his many children. It was a tough time for cacao in Mexico, and most of the kids quickly cut down the old trees and replaced them with coffee, sugarcane, or whatever crop was paying the highest price at the time.

But Anselmo never touched the old trees on his seventy-five acres. "It wasn't a business," Pablo explains. "Cacao was very romantic for my grandfather." His grandmother even started a boutique chocolate business, using the fifty-year-old Lehmann mills and melangeurs. Eventually, word of this actually got back to the president of Lehmann in Germany, who made the trip to Soconusco and offered to buy back the machines for the company's museum. Anselmo politely refused, and here they remain, still functional.

Eventually, the orchard fell to Pablo's father and entered a period of benign neglect. Ignored, it reverted to jungle, as happens to any piece of ground in one of the hottest and wettest places on earth. But cacao trees don't die easily, and a couple of years ago, Pablo decided to revive the old garden. Of the fifty acres of surviving cacao, he's hacked back the jungle on half. "Want to see?" he asks.

We do.

As Pablo walks us through the living time capsule, I can feel my excitement rising. Most working cacao farms experienced constant introductions of new hybrid varieties throughout the twentieth and twenty-first centuries. Even heirlooms in the vicinity would cross-pollinate with the introductions, so their seeds would yield hybrids. But here? All pure prewar cacao. Every one of these centenarians could be the next breakout heirloom star. I look for identifying signs or labels on the trees, but I see nothing. "How do you keep track of which variety is which?" I ask.

Pablo levels his gaze at me. "We don't."

Slowly, understanding dawns on me. "Oh, you have no idea what's what?"

"Nope." He shrugs and throws up his arms with a smile.

"Have you done any genetic testing?"

"No. Too expensive."

"Would you like to?"

"Yeah, for sure. So I can identify which trees have the best flavor. Chocolate is my passion!"

Pablo is a chemical engineer in Mexico City, but he's been playing around with his cacao, making chocolate on tabletop equipment. Later, when he slides us some samples, I'm blown away. This wasn't chocolate made from two or three varieties of cacao, this was made from hundreds.

Suddenly Alejandro's eyes fall on one particular tree and he drops to his knees in reverence. "Lagardo!" he squeaks, gazing longingly at two bizarre pods dangling from a branch. They look like dinosaur eggs. Brick red, long and skinny, with a tapering tip, patinated skin, and raised ridges, as if the five plates of the husk had been welded together. "Look at that!" he coos. "It's mesmerizing!" Although all the native cacaos of Mexico are classified as Criollos, Alejandro explains, most of them don't look wildly different from other cacao. "But this checks all the boxes! Corrugated skin, very long lizard tail, very long pod, very round seeds, most of them white. It doesn't get any more heirloom than this!"

This is exactly what we're here for. We tuck away some samples and continue on through the garden, an embarrassment of riches awaiting us. And as we reach the crumbling brick wall and turn to walk the perimeter, I realize we are walking a perfect metaphor. This land is one giant secret garden of heirloom cacao, isolated from the world, struggling to survive. The garden is unsung, underfunded, covered in vines. But it's filled with living treasures. And they aren't getting any younger.

The Real White Chocolate

One of the surest ways to tell a pretender from a real chocophile is their enthusiasm for white chocolate. This pale companion to true chocolate is made from cocoa butter, the natural fat in chocolate, and sugar. It became possible during the industrial revolution, when machines were invented that could separate the solids in cacao beans from the fat. The solids became known as *cocoa powder*, a useful industrial product that contains the flavorful compounds of chocolate but none of the richness, and the fat became known as *cocoa butter*, a substance in great demand in both the food and cosmetics industries.

Cocoa butter possesses the neat trick of being solid at room temperature but liquid at body temperature, the quality that has kept trillions of M&Ms from melting until they hit your mouth. It also provides great texture for skin care products. But it doesn't have much flavor of its own. So white chocolate doesn't taste like chocolate at all; just the sugar and vanilla it's usually flavored with.

Chocoholics tend to dismiss white chocolate out of hand, and chalk up its existence to a historical misconception. They will tell you that, yes, Mexico was full of references to white cacao in the old days, but this had nothing to do with white chocolate. Instead, it referred to the white-beaned varieties of Criollo prized by the peoples of Mesoamerica for millennia. In contrast to most cacao, which has purple beans that make bitter, astringent chocolate, Criollo has had the bitter, purple-colored compounds bred out of it. Its beans are pale, only slightly bitter, and highly prized, and the chocolate made from it looks more like milk chocolate than dark chocolate.

But these armchair pros are only partially correct. Yes, white-beaned Criollo is still revered in Mexico and elsewhere. But in the traditional chocolate heartland of Oaxaca, Tabasco, and Chiapas, *white cacao* usually refers to a different tree altogether: *Theobroma bicolor*, a close cousin to *Theobroma cacao*, also known in the region as pataxte.

Pataxte is cacao's less flashy partner, and it has always played a supporting role in Mexico's traditional beverage culture. Like cacao, it has large seed-filled pods, but the pods hang from the branch ends, not the trunks. They have strange patterns etched into the husks, which makes them look like undersea sponges. Its white beans have less fat than cacao and a milder taste, more nutty than chocolatey, but they have a distinctness all their own.

As cacao became a global commodity, pataxte was left behind, forgotten save for cultural pockets that maintained the old tradition of mixing it with cacao. Only a handful of people in the world still grow it commercially. Its last refuge is in the hills of the Chinantla, a remote region of Oaxaca where the Chinantec people have resisted modernization, and even there, only a few tons a year is produced.

But now pataxte is having a moment, buoyed by the rising interest in Mexico's ancient food traditions. Look for it in the chocolate drinks served on the streets of Oaxaca City, and increasingly in a few North American chocolate bars and online stores. Feel free to direct anyone wanting to experience "real" white chocolate its way.

24

The Saga of Almendra Blanca
Chiapas and Tabasco, Mexico, 2023

Cacao hunting in Mexico means submitting yourself to bus hell. Big buses, minibuses, colectivos, plus a whole lot of privately negotiated taxis, and the occasional back of a truck, choking on dust. In our quest to track down the cream of Mexico's cacao crop for the Heirloom Cacao Preservation Fund, Alejandro Zamorano, Alyssa D'Adamo, and I got painfully familiar with all of them, even though we were traversing just three states: Oaxaca, Tabasco, and Chiapas.

Oaxaca is mostly for cultural reasons. It's the place where so many of Mexico's homegrown arts and traditions have reached their most vibrant expression, chocolate among them, and the place where they're best preserved. If you want to understand how cacao has been consumed and considered for centuries, you go to Oaxaca. But the state itself produces barely a smidge of the stuff. More than 99 percent comes from its two sister states down at the tail end of Mexico.

And they couldn't be more different. I think of Tabasco as the Louisiana of Mexico: a hot, steamy swamp on the Gulf of Mexico steeped in strong local traditions and catapulted out of poverty in the late twentieth century by the discovery of vast reserves of oil just offshore. Tabasco is now one of Mexico's wealthiest states, a flat coastal plain with lots of industry. Physically and demographically, it's relatively homogenous.

Chiapas is the opposite, a jumble of mountains, microclimates, and cultures, most of them poor. So when the Mexican government decided to modernize its cacao industry in the late twentieth century, it managed to get most of Tabasco's cacaoteros, as they're called, to replace their relic varieties with modern high-performance ones, and to convert to chemical-intensive techniques. But it barely made inroads in Chiapas.

The reasons run deep. Chiapas is the home of the Zapatista movement. The Indigenous cacaoteros of Chiapas have a strong and well-earned distrust of the federal government. And along with that, an unshakable faith in the value of tradition and continuity. "It would be a sin to cut down trees my great-grandfather planted," one farmer tells us.

But it was also just smart farming. The new government strains were bred for success on nice, flat research-station plots whose conditions bore little resemblance to the hardscrabble realities of Soconusco hill farms, and the farmers knew it. "What works at their research station doesn't work at my farm, two hundred meters higher and on the other side of the mountain," says the farmer. And the reason his trees *do* work is because he and his family have been planting them from seed, generation after generation, which allows the genetics to continually adapt to the conditions. In Soconusco, the sweet spot is at three hundred to five hundred meters of altitude, too high and dry for the fungal diseases that prey on cacao at lower altitudes, but still in the cacao comfort zone.

Chiapas also resisted the push to grow cacao in the same way as other industrial crops, in neat, orderly rows. To walk the steep slopes of Finca Cuatro Hermanos, a fifty-acre organic farm that has become a prized source for Mexico's handful of bean-to-bar chocolate makers, is to climb through a food forest of cacao, coffee, avocado, mango, banana, and zapote, hopping from rock to rock across babbling brooks. Vanilla orchids cling to the trees. Dogs follow behind you on the footpaths, but no machinery can. The grandsons of the original four brothers now do the harvesting, cracking pods on the slopes, filling sacks with wet beans, and carrying them down the precipitous paths with tumplines on their foreheads.

It's beautiful and inspiring . . . and, unexpectedly, good business. What started as simple obstinance has now come full circle and is looking very much like the future of cacao farming. First Mexico's bean-to-bar makers, then the world's: everybody wants these beans.

The hiccup, once again, was fermentation. Because in Mexico almost all cacao is consumed as sweet drinking chocolate, which doesn't require beans with beautiful flavor, cacaoteros never bothered fermenting at all. They just washed and dried the beans and sold them cheap. But then Mexico's first bean-to-bar start-ups began reaching out, offering to pay six dollars per kilo for well-fermented beans, instead of the three dollars per kilo for lavado—washed. And then exporters like Alejandro began offering nine dollars and up. And the farmers caught on fast. "I mean, even five years ago, you could count on both hands the number of farmers thinking outside the box and trying to do things differently," Alejandro says. Now you'd need a lot more hands and feet.

What makes these beans so desirable is that they are Criollo, the endemic variety of Mexico and Central America. But not just any Criollo is worth nine dollars a kilo. It has to be white-beaned, what people in Mexico call "Almendra Blanca." Those beans have been a long-standing obsession in the region. Some even call it a fetish. While Almendra Blanca is undeniably smooth and mild, some actually prefer the chocolatey complexity and bitter backbeat of darker beans with more polyphenols.

Fetish or not, the basics of Almendra Blanca are well established. In prehistory, Criollo developed from earlier strains of cacao in Colombia and Venezuela, as cacao made its way up into Mesoamerica, passed from hand to hand. In their ongoing quest for the ultimate cup of chocolate, people kept planting the seeds from their favorite trees, the ones that tended to be less bitter and astringent.

That nastiness is built into cacao seeds as a survival mechanism, to keep animals from nibbling on them, and it comes in the form of polyphenol compounds that happen to be purple. Most cacao seeds are deep purple and very bitter. But over the millennia, as the least-bitter cacao was selected again and again, it became pale and deliciously nutty. Not all Criollo is pale—some is a lovely light lavender—but the whiter the bean, the more those in the know want it.

Almendra Blanca is changing the fortunes of cacaoteros in Chiapas and everywhere else they have access to it. The most famous of all Almendra Blancas is found due north of Soconusco, on the opposite coast of Mexico, in La Chontalpa, the center of Tabasco's cacao industry. Yes, Chontalpa long ago hitched its wagon to the usual modern hybrids. But one family is bucking the trend.

θ

"We're sort of hippies," explains Alma Delia Magaña Peralta as she leads me through Finca Las Delias, her family's 2,400-tree biodynamic cacao orchard. "Maybe the only hippies in Tabasco." Alma, with her yoga pants and bio ways, long black hair pulled back in a scrunchie as she plucks a pod and cuts it in half, is definitely an aberration.

She holds out the half-pod to me. It's full of beans white as cream. Almost all the cacao trees at Finca Las Delias are Almendra Blanca, interspersed with a handful of other varieties for diversity, as well as an abundance of shade trees and other fruit crops—a classic biodynamic fruit forest. Alma is new to farming, and still in her twenties, having returned home during the pandemic after several years working as an architect in cities all over Mexico. Drawn to the cacao trees her mother had recently planted as an experiment, she soon took to the rhythms of farming as if born to it—which she kind of was. It was just down the road, at another finca, that her great-aunt first brought Almendra Blanca to the world.

The story begins in the 1940s, when a man named Carlos Echeverria inherited an abandoned farm scattered with overgrown cacao trees. He named it Finca La Joya. As you'd expect in a region that had been growing Criollo cacao since antiquity, and where international hybrids hadn't yet arrived, many were white-beaned. Carlos began experimenting, selecting his favorites for propagation, searching for the perfect combination of flavor and vigor, and also doing something unheard of in Tabasco: grafting the trees onto better rootstock to improve their yield.

Eventually, he landed on a tree that knocked it out of the park on both flavor and productivity and began cloning it, the first true white-beaned varietal. He named it Carmelo.

And it was awesome. Intensely aromatic when properly fermented, gentle on the palate, supremely buttery, a good producer. But at the time, Mexico had no interest in well-fermented cacao, and Carmelo stayed a local oddity. Eventually, Carlos died and the farm passed to his daughter, Clara Echeverria. And she would turn out to be a force of nature.

In the 1980s, the fine-chocolate craze surged to life in Europe. Companies like Bonnat and Valrhona began marketing single-origin bars from regions like Chuao, and Clara Echeverria realized this was her natural audience. She was a classy cacaotera with a stately ranch, an excellent handler of trees and fermentation protocols, and Finca La Joya became Mexico's first famed single-origin, and its first to win the top prize at the international Cacao of Excellence Awards. Scientists and chocolate-industry bigwigs came to stay at Finca La Joya, which accrued the cachet of a top wine estate.

And prices exploded. Eleven dollars per kilo for Carmelo beans. Then even more. A kind of tulipomania took hold. Everyone in the region wanted to plant Carmelo trees and get in on the game. Millions of dollars were raised by syndicates so they could build nurseries, propagate trees, sell the seedlings, and even buy the cacao, process it, and sell it. La Chontalpa bet everything it had on Carmelo.

And then it all came crashing down. A lot of it was simple supply and demand. As more and more farms came online, a glut of Carmelo hit the market. Prices tanked.

But there was more to it. The more people tasted it, the more they decided maybe Carmelo wasn't all it was cracked up to be.

A lot of it just didn't taste as good as Finca La Joya's, for reasons that would not have surprised anyone in the wine business. It wasn't just the genetics of the trees. It was the terroir of the place. Maybe it was Finca La Joya's soil, or environment, or Clara's management and fermentation skills. Whatever the case, Carmelo's reputation declined. The bubble burst.

The good times didn't even last at Finca La Joya. Clara died in 2013, the family squabbled over the ranch, the heirs didn't keep up the orchard, and a few years ago Finca La Joya was abandoned. We stood outside its locked gate and flew a drone over the overgrown ruins, a source of profound heartache to the remaining family members.

But now the legacy of Finca La Joya is growing again—grafted, literally, from the original rootstock. A few years ago, Clara's niece, Alma's mom, took grafts from the trees and started her own orchard in honor of her aunt Clarita. It was just a pet project, and Alma wasn't involved—she was off in the city being an architect, and her mom was pretty sure she'd never come back. Then, in 2020, Covid struck and Alma did come back—and fell in love with cacao farming.

It was a steep learning curve, she admits. Farming biodynamically means eschewing chemicals and learning to prune and augment the soil in ways that trace the seasonal rhythms. It means paying close attention to each individual tree and what it needs. It means accepting that disease is going to take out a certain number of your trees.

And learning to ferment your beans, when you never grew up around cacao, can be a strange education. "When I started," Alma says, "I couldn't make any connection between what was a good smell in the beans and what was a bad one. For me, everything was bad, because it smelled like vinegar!" But after tasting enough of the chocolate, she began using a lighter hand with fermentation, which suits such gentle beans, and today her beans have brought Carmelo's reputation back to its heyday. They command some of the highest prices in the world, and thus far have been snapped up by Mexico's new bean-to-bar chocolate makers before they could even make it out of the country.

For our work with the Heirloom Cacao Preservation Fund, it was a no-brainer. Genetically and visually distinct, great-tasting beans that can't be found anywhere else? Sign them up.

If only it were always that easy. If I've given the impression that wrangling up new candidates for Heirloom Cacao consideration is a walk in the park, Modelo in hand, please allow me to correct the record. Let me tell you about the White Jaguar.

25

In Search of the White Jaguar

Chiapas, Mexico, 2023

T he quest for forgotten cacao is largely a game of dead ends. For every clue that leads to an inspiring cacaotera and awesome beans, five end in nothingness. The farm has been cut down, or the cultivars turn out to be common ones introduced all over the world in the 1990s, or the old farmer has zero interest in doing the fermentation required to make great beans, preferring to just sell cheap into the lavado market and be done with it.

Or, worse, it's simply too dangerous to get to the trees. I had thought my brushes with that sort of lawlessness had ended with my last flight out of Bolivia. But I was wrong.

Just as Belize has its Maya Mountains, and Guatemala its Maya Biosphere Reserve, Mexico has Montes Azules Biosphere Reserve, its last large tract of high-quality rainforest, running along the Chiapas-Guatemala border and actually contiguous with the Guatemalan reserves. The area's remoteness and impenetrability have made it the last reserve for all sorts of plants, animals, *and people* who don't want to be found.

Five centuries ago, that included the Lacandon Maya, the last group of Maya who refused to submit to the Spanish invaders. In 1586, after years of skirmishes, they retreated deep into the jungle, built a community of about one hundred houses, and lived off the land, trading grudgingly—but more often fighting—with neighboring "domesticated" Maya communities. They named their settlement Sac Balam, or White Jaguar.

For a century, Sac Balam maintained its fierce independence, but in 1695 the Spanish finally forced it to integrate. They cleared the entire town, the jungle quickly reclaimed it, and no archaeologist has been able to rediscover the site, despite multiple expeditions.

Another holdout long suspected to be harbored by the Lacandon jungle is ancient Criollo. As in Belize and Guatemala, there's nowhere better for the original strains to avoid cross-pollination with introduced hybrids.

This, at least, was the hunch of Carlos Avendaño Arrazate and Alexander Mendoza López, two cacao experts at Mexico's National Institute for Forestry, Agriculture and Livestock Research. The institute maintains a giant clonal garden of Mexican cacao varieties at its field station in Soconusco, a kind of genetic library that it offers to cacao farmers who wish to incorporate a wider range of genetics into their farms. Although the institute had many varieties with a percentage of Criollo parentage, the two scientists had long dreamed of adding pure, ancient Criollo to the mix, but it had eluded them. That part of Mexico's past seemed to have closed.

They knew the Lacandon jungle was the one place they might be able to find it, and in 2010, they raised the funds for a collecting expedition. After days of exploration and conversations with the Zapatista farmers who control the area, they managed to find twenty-three trees. They were tall and spindly, with strange and small pods, both red ones and yellow ones. The beans were extremely white. They were clearly relic Criollos, likely dating back to ancient times. In a nod to the history of the region, they named the variety Sac Balam.

Back at their research station in Soconusco, they germinated a number of seeds. But the seedlings all died. Like its namesake, the White Jaguar didn't like being removed from the jungle.

But Alexander had slightly better luck at his house in Soconusco. He'd planted ten seeds from the original pods, and a single one of those seedlings survived. For ten years, he coaxed the tree along, until it finally produced a single pod. Then it, too, died. But he planted the seeds from that last pod at a friend's cacao farm, and three of those trees are alive today. But that is Sac Balam's only fingerhold on survival outside the Lacandon jungle.

For years, Alexander had wanted to revisit the jungle to get new samples, to expand the precariously narrow genetic bottleneck of the three surviving trees. And our HCP expedition finally gave him an opportunity—and funding. Permissions to cross the area were obtained from the local Zapatistas, an important consideration in this rough part of Chiapas. The Marxist-leaning Zapatistas took over many parts of Chiapas in their 1994 uprising, calling for land reforms and greater rights for Indigenous groups. Although the army drove them out of the main cities, they still control much of the Chiapas countryside, and they have morphed into a political party with tremendous popular support. They don't take kindly to mysterious foreigners showing up unannounced, so we carefully laid the groundwork.

Still, as we depart San Cristóbal de las Casas, the capital of Chiapas, early in the morning and make the eight-hour trip to the Lacandon jungle, tensions are simmering across the region. Two hours after we leave San Cristóbal, the local leader of the artisans' guild—which tightly controls the lucrative crafts trade—is gunned down by motorcyclists, and in response shootings and fires flare across the state as rival cartels settle scores.

Under the circumstances, the jungle feels like the best place anyone could be, and the feeling grows as we roll past idyllic communities of clear streams, maize-covered hillsides, and playing children. As evening falls, we're greeted warmly by our Zapatista hosts and share a dinner of extremely chewy steak, then crash at a nearby river lodge. Living the campesino dream, more or less.

But the feeling doesn't last. The next morning we're supposed to head to the jungle at four thirty, but our guides never show up. Six o'clock, seven . . . eight. Something has spooked them.

As we sit around trying to decide if we, too, should be spooked, our luck turns. A worker at the lodge overhears us talking about wild cacao and says he knows where to find a tree, just up the trail. Did we want to take a look?

Hell yes.

He leads us up the trail into a lost world of thundering waterfalls and dripping limestone caves. Bats flit around us. Mosquitoes swarm. At the base of a giant cliff, he stops and points. "Cacao!"

Sure enough. The tree is about twenty-five feet tall, skinny, no branches until way up. There are also no pods, but Alexander excitedly confirms its identity. Then he spots a second tree ten yards away. Then a rosita de cacao tree close by. He says the trees often grow together. The flowers have been used to flavor cacao drinks and produce a better froth since ancient times, and the branching sticks make natural molinillos—the wooden whisks used for raising a nice head of froth.

A nice find. We take a leaf for genetic sequencing. But with no pods, it's not going to help us make more Sac Balam. We line up new guides, hop into the back of a pickup, and head for the area where Alexander thinks he found the trees thirteen years ago. The rutted road bumps along through forested hills and subsistence farms being hacked out of the jungle. But as we head deeper into the river valley, our new guides get increasingly nervous. Eventually, we hunker down for a conference. "From here forward," they explain, "do NOT take photos of any people you see!"

So many questions. But we can't get any specifics out of them. "Just don't take photos of anything except cacao trees!"

Okay, no problem. That's why we're here.

But as we continue, the looks I'm getting from the farmers we pass just don't feel right. The whole timbre of the day shades in the wrong direction, and I start to wonder about risk and reward. Then some locals outside a hut flag down our truck, and everyone gathers for an emergency strategy session.

Finally, we get some info. The deep jungle where we're headed has recently been taken over by strangers. No one exactly understands where they came from, but they carved out a settlement and began farming poppies for heroin production. They even cut landing strips so planes could fly in and out. And our friends want no part of them.

"But you guys are Zapatistas!" I protest. "You're paramilitary!"

Our friends shake their heads. No, these guys are scary. And they have serious firepower. And serious friends. There's no getting rid of them.

And it gets even weirder. Whoever these narcotraffickers are, they aren't your modern city gang members. No, they are some cult that practices animal sacrifices. Everyone had hoped that they would be in a different part of their territory today, and we'd be able to slip by, but unfortunately, as it turns out, they are holding one of their ceremonial sacrifices today right on the road up ahead. And if strangers with cameras appear out of nowhere, well . . . disaster.

The pall of silence lasts a few seconds while we all contemplate the world we're in, and then one of our hosts perks up. "But if you still want to try, we can see what happens."

It's not exactly a tough call. We turn the truck around and rattle off the way we came. I'm stunned that the drug trade has yet again crossed my path, and saddened again by the global instabilities racking Latin America. None of this can be fixed by chocolate, of course. But as we feed back into the system, I see more than ever the importance of nurturing the parts of it that are working. We need these beacons of hope in the darkening forest.

26

The Metaphysics of Chocolate

Mexico City and Oaxaca, Mexico, 2023

S tart at the great square of the Zócalo, heart of Mexico City, where it all began. Five hundred years ago, when the city was known as Tenochtitlán, a billion beans spilled from its coffers and cacao became something new. To take stock of what it has been, and what it might become next, you could do worse than stand here, beside the ghosts of the Mexica, in what is still the center of Mesoamerican power.

Now wander west, past the Palacio de Bellas Artes and the Diego Rivera murals, hang a left at the Monument to the Mexican Revolution, and find your way down a charming side street to the ornate stone archways and wrought-iron balconies of MuCho, the Museum of Chocolate.

The first thing you notice about MuCho is the building: a 1909 gem from Mexico's Porfirian period. That's how it all began for Ana Rita García Lascuráin, a well-known Mexico City architect. "I had the job to restore this property, which was in a part of the city that was very run-down back in 2010," she says as she ushers me into the central courtyard, which is reverberating with laughter and the low crunch of stone on stone as five kneeling visitors try their hand at metates, smearing a chocolatey mess across the stones and themselves. Ana's got a deep, throaty voice and a powerful presence, and I could easily see her holding forth with a cigarette in one hand and a mezcal in the other. "And as we started working on the reconstruction of this beautiful house, we realized that the neighborhood had a long-standing history of culture and diversity."

It seemed obvious that the house should become a cultural center of some kind, and Ana and her circle quickly homed in on chocolate as a perfect focus, because, well, of course. "Chocolate is so metaphysical" is how Ana puts it. "In the end, it's such a pleasurable thing, and so related to memories. When we taste it and smell it, each one of us goes back in time to a certain moment or a certain place or a certain experience. And I think there are very few sensorial experiences that do that for you."

So chocolate's inherent meaningfulness seemed like a good way to get people in the door, but the opportunity Ana saw was much larger than that. "Chocolate has been in Mexico for over four thousand years, but there was no place to educate about it. And we realized that it was an opportunity to found a cultural institution that would open its doors to everybody and could communicate all kinds of topics around cacao and chocolate and Mexican history. So it started as an experiment with friends that were anthropologists, historians, artists, designers, architects, and it became this ongoing experience of collective culture making."

I mull that idea of collective culture making as we tour MuCho's three stories of exhibits, squeezed into a warren of

small spaces that feels less like a museum than like some chocolate fanatic's private home. We climb the staircase past the
antique cacao mill and duck through rooms that suck you into
the sociological sweep of this powerful substance. There are
dioramas of cacao's role in the forest, of prehistoric Mesoamerican families making chocolate, of Maya and Mexica cacao
culture, of the first contact with the conquistadores. The walls
and even the ceilings are festooned with metates and molinillos
of all shapes and sizes, poems in Nahuatl and Spanish, archival
photographs of life on old cacao farms, extraordinary collections
of chocolate packaging and advertising and graphic design from
the beginnings of the industrial era to the modern day. There's
chocolate sculpture, a three-story abstract chocolate mural in the
courtyard, and a closet wallpapered with 2,981 discs of MuCho's
own drinking chocolate. It's an almost cubist effort to capture
"the elegance of the spirit and the objects," as Ana puts it.

It all starts to feel like an unpacking of my head, of all the
impressions that have formed as I've tracked the flow of cacao
through time and place. For people new to the subject, tourists
just looking to score a tasty treat, it must be a revelation. Chocolate is the lure, but soon they're drawn into a funhouse of history
and ritual and capitalism, and they're unexpectedly thinking
about farming and colonialism and family and the means of
production. They come for chocolate, and they get Mexico.

They also get MuCho's own chocolate bars, which turn out
to be some of the best in Mexico. In 2015, Ana began working
directly with Mexican farms producing the top heirloom beans.
Each gets their own small-batch bar, made by MuCho's in-house
chocolate maker in an antique mold that mirrors the building.
So after the master class on what chocolate has been to so many
different people, visitors finish with a very direct experience of

what chocolate can be right now. In other words, yes, in all the classic ways, MuCho is a museum of Mexico's storied past. But it's also a museum of the future.

"It's very hard to think about culture in a static way," Ana tells me as we nibble squares from each bar. "I mean, we're a museum, we're all about preserving tradition. But you can't force traditions. We also want to inspire new ideas, new traditions that will be the backbone of future generations."

It's a captivating notion. All old traditions were new once. And some of the best traditions arise when new generations take the old ones, the things that gave structure and a sense of place and continuity to their early lives, and reinterpret them to make them meaningful going forward. It happens with all traditions that stay vibrant, and it is happening now with chocolate.

Step out of the Museum of Chocolate, wander a few blocks south, and you may find your way to a little circular plaza where two side streets meet, filled with café tables and jacaranda trees silently sprinkling pink confetti over the scene. On one side of this plaza, the people are drinking coffee. On the other side, a few countercultural souls sit outside a tiny shop beneath a banner proclaiming in bold lettering ¡POR UN FUTURO FRATERNO Y SOLIDARIO! They are drinking chocolate. But the chocolate isn't like that found in the thousands of other chocolaterías in Mexico City. The cacao is sourced entirely from small farmers in Mexico, it's made into chocolate by hand in the micro factory in the back of the shop, and most of it is fermented to perfection. In short, it's some of the most beautiful drinking chocolate you'll find, and many people in Mexico City have no idea what to make of it.

The shop is called La Rifa, and the revolutionary fervor continues as you step inside. CHOCOLATE IS FOR THE BODY, announces the wall above the counter. FOAM IS FOR THE SOUL. You can take that foamy chocolate sweet or bitter, con agua or leche, with chilies or cardamom or straight up.

I order mine strong and straight and hold down a table out front, guarding my foam from stray jacaranda petals until La Rifa's proprietors, Mónica Lozano and Daniel Reza, escape to join me. Daniel shows me his tattoos—corn on one forearm, a cacao flower on the other, the yin and yang of Mexican culinary mythology—and explains that they launched La Rifa in 2012 as a tiny factory to address a fundamental issue: the chocolate in Mexico City sucked. It was all being mass produced by a handful of big corporations with very low standards. But quickly, their quest to make better chocolate led them down the same rabbit hole as so many other people in this book. They needed better raw material, which meant cutting out the middlemen and going straight to the farmers.

"We had the technical knowledge of how to make chocolate," says Mónica, "but we wanted to know more about the bean itself, so we could better understand what we were doing. We started traveling to Tabasco and Chiapas. And somebody knew somebody who knew somebody."

The farmers welcomed new buyers who were willing to pay higher prices than the coyotes they usually dealt with, but they were still suspicious, Mónica admits. "At first, they were confused, because we were very young, and we were from the city, and we wanted to visit the cacao farms and learn to work with the beans. Daniel was working in the fermentation area with one of the families, and they were like, 'Why do you want to know all of this? Like, where is this interest coming from?'"

But as they stuck with it, the farmers came to trust them and to value the relationship-driven business partnership, long traditional in Mexican culture, and they soon found themselves enmeshed in "one big network of reciprocity," as Mónica puts it. "And the beautiful thing was that they were open with us. They opened their cacao farms, and they were open with their knowledge and traditions. We'd had no idea how much work went into harvesting cacao."

They began producing single-origin bars with each of their farming partners and selling them throughout Mexico City. Then they added chocolate festivals, salons, and their café to the mix, trying to jump-start a culture of appreciation.

There's no saying whether they'll succeed. They have their appreciators, for sure, but La Rifa and MuCho are still very much outliers in a market that caters to sweet tooths. Mexico City does not seem like a city on the verge of becoming a bean-to-bar bastion. If anything, it's a reminder that chocolate is still a big business.

No, when the revolution comes, it will not be born here in the heart of the empire. In my experience, almost all good ideas, authentic insights, start in the provinces. And so will this one. So we head south, full circle, and end right where this book began. In Oaxaca.

"I think cacao saved me," says Flor Heras. We're sitting in her tiny chocolate shop on a backstreet of Oaxaca City, sipping on insanely good, velvety-smooth iced mochas. It's such an unexpected thing to say in a conversation about her chocolate brand, Reina Negra, that at first I think I've misunderstood. But then she says it again, fighting back tears. "Cacao was in my blood.

I tried to run away. But I think it was just a question of time before I came back, because it could save me from a very hard part of my life. And when I came back to chocolate, I came back to my grandma."

Flor has dark hair and deep-set eyes that one would describe as chocolatey if one weren't writing a book about chocolate. She designs all her own packaging, bright Matisse-like prints of animals and tropical tropes, and she has a graphic designer's penchant for tattoos and floral-print blouses. Flor says Reina Negra represents the spirit of cacao itself, and all the women who have passed that spirit along. "For me, Reina Negra is everywhere. She can be in Peru. She can be in Mexico. She can be in Africa. Sometimes she's a spirit, sometimes she's a jaguar, sometimes she's a monkey. She connects all these traditions."

Flor grew up immersed in the world of chocolate, too close to do anything other than take it for granted. Her grandmother had ten children but was widowed at an early age. To survive, she owned a small grocery store and scraped by, selling anything she could. Flor says she was a tough old bird. "She used to say she would have sold herself if she wasn't too old! She couldn't hug you, but she could feed you. When you arrived at her home, the first question was always, 'Did you eat?' And she always had something to give you."

By the time Flor's generation came along, her grandmother had become known for her handmade discs of drinking chocolate, and she put Flor and her cousins to work producing them. "I remember making chocolate with her, just being happy with her. Peeling the cacao, roasting the cacao, eating tortillas. We were loud and a little bit mischievous. It was a way to keep us entertained. But I think it was also a way to heal herself, to bring the family together."

Eventually, Flor's father decided to turn the family's chocolate-making expertise into a full-blown company, launching a brand called El Rito that put higher-quality drinking chocolate into supermarkets across Mexico. It was mass-produced, but a step above the discs one would buy on the street. He often took along Flor and her sister on business trips. "So I was in the cacao industry," she says, "but just as the daughter of the owner. You know, playing in the factory."

As an adult, she focused on art and graphic design, never realizing chocolate still had a hold on her soul until a crisis hit. "When I was twenty-seven, I had a breakdown," says Flor, who is now in her mid-thirties. Newly divorced, rudderless, she felt like her life was falling apart. "My dad told me I just had to get away for a while. So I went to Vienna and stayed with a friend for a couple of months. And it was there that I discovered all these bean-to-bar chocolates."

She found the chocolate incredibly delicious, better than any she'd known back home. But she found the labels infuriating. "The funny part was that I read that the chocolate was from Austria. And I felt like, 'Austria doesn't have cacao! So how can they say it's Austrian chocolate?' And all the labels that I read said the cacao was from Africa, from Costa Rica, from Panama, not from Mexico. So I felt there was something missing. Because we have cacao! But how I can make bars with this quality?"

She returned to Mexico determined to figure that out. She opened the shop in Oaxaca City, selling drinking chocolate and all the El Rito products. But to her surprise, a lot of the clientele walking in the door weren't asking for the traditional high-sugar, low-chocolate kind. Oaxaca City draws a sophisticated crowd of visitors, both international and domestic, and they were looking for drinks with more cacao, better flavor, less sugar. They were also looking for eating chocolate. That gave her the confidence to launch Reina Negra, one of the first bean-to-bar chocolates in Mexico using high-quality heirloom cacao and creative inclusions like mango, mezcal, and pataxte. "It's a brand that takes my family roots in cacao and transforms it for new generations," she says. "Young people like me who want to eat more chocolate but also connect with their traditions."

That need to connect, to heal, caught her by surprise as she began visiting the Oaxaca countryside in search of sources of heirloom cacao and pataxte. "When you're in the fields, there's something in the air. In the colors, the plants, the water, even the people. It's different . . . I can't explain it."

Flor pauses and looks us over, deciding how frankly to speak. I think I know what's coming, having seen it now from so many cacao devotees in so many places. You can't explain the truth of chocolate without getting, as Ana Rita García Lascuráin would say, metaphysical. She decides we can handle it. "There's this *energy*," she says. "Call it whatever you want. There's this *essence* in the plants, and also in the chocolate. You know, my rational mind tells me we like chocolate because it has dopamine and theobromine and so on, but my heart is like, 'You are healing in this place.' And that surprised me. It's very deep, the connection we have with this plant."

That sacramental quality was something the Maya and Mexica and Zapotec understood instinctively. But the beauty of chocolate is that it brings the holy Daime to you wherever you are. That connection may have been lost for a few generations, but now people everywhere seem to be finding it again. To that hopeful awakening we now turn for one last bit of ceremony.

Ritual

New Hampshire, USA, 2023

The first thing I notice as I walk up to the glass window of the tiny shop is an etching of a lion tangoing with a cacao pod. When I open the door and step inside, a wave of chocolate scent hits me. I move past the little tile tables to the glass counter, with its display of truffles, bonbons, and edible art, and order a drinking chocolate from Richard Tango-Lowy, the proprietor of Dancing Lion Chocolate in Manchester, New Hampshire. ("Tango as in the dance, and Lowy means 'lion' in Romanian" is how he explains the name.)

Rich is a former physicist who took a chocolate-making class, fell in love with the craft, and changed career paths. He's now one of the world's great chocolatiers, and one of the few who makes his own chocolate from the beans—although that work is now in the hands of Shaman Marlin, Jacob Marlin's son, currently scooting around the back kitchen in a bandanna with some new test batches of beans. Rich got to know Jacob through the Heirloom Cacao Preservation Fund, where he's a board member and, as of 2024, the new president.

As Rich starts to froth up a storm behind the counter, I have a seat at one of the tables and think about ceremony. A few years ago, something new began bubbling up in the world of chocolate. Actually, what made it interesting was that it *wasn't* the classic world of chocolate. Yoga and mindfulness practitioners began incorporating cacao ceremonies into their practices. Now you can "sit in ceremony" with self-styled cacao shamans all over the world and let a cup of "ceremonial-grade cacao" open your apertures. The style varies from place to place, but generally involves making and sipping a cup of chocolate while thinking a lot about intentionality. Chanting optional.

It would be easy to make fun of some of these operations, especially when the operators are gringo gurus claiming special powers for their ceremonial-grade stuff and charging a fortune for it. I myself find no need to enrobe my chakras in guru-approved chocolate. But I actually like the trend. Chocolate is returning to its roots. For thousands of years before it became candy, cacao was medicine. It was all ceremonial-grade.

Rich sets a steaming bowl of chocolate before me. Yes, bowl. He serves all his drinking chocolate in ceramic bowls made by a local potter. It's part of his Japan-inspired aesthetic. Minimal glitz, barely sweet sweets, and fine attention to simple details. "Once we made chocolate hearts for Valentine's Day," he tells me, "and they were beautiful. But I could tell my other chocolatier wasn't happy with them, and I wasn't happy either. I mean, they were gorgeous, but they just weren't right. And we were sitting here having tea one morning, and she said, 'We need to break the hearts.' And I said, 'Yeah.' So we went in there and took all the hearts and just *smashed* them, and then glued them back together. And they were beautiful. And that's what they needed."

The pottery bowls do more than add an artisanal flair to the experience, Rich says. "This place is probably a little bit more traditional Japanese teahouse than anything else. We don't allow cell phone conversations. You're here to pay attention. And the cool thing about the bowls is you can't drink from a bowl and *not* pay attention."

Indeed, it's true. I could lift up the bowl with one hand, but it would be awkward, so I end up using two, cradling it all the way to my mouth. And for a moment, my world is foam.

"We learned this years ago," Rich continues. "People would come in, and they'd be busy, but when you pick up a bowl, you have to stop. These two guys came in, obviously lawyers, and they took over a table and had papers everywhere. And they'd be talking and talking, and then it would get quiet, and I'd look up. And they'd both be drinking from their bowls. And there'd be fifteen seconds of *nothing*. And then they'd go back to work."

I can't help thinking of the Japanese tea ceremony, that other celebration of foam and stillness. The ritual of the tea ceremony is, in the great description of Okakura Kakuzo in *The Book of Tea*, "founded on the adoration of the beautiful among the sordid facts of everyday existence." In the simplicity of sitting in the tea hut, boiling water and whipping powdered matcha into a jade-green froth, you learn to see, in its impermanence, the grace of the tiny good thing.

Cacao serves up the same. That quality is acknowledged right in the name of one of the best new bean-to-bar makers, Utah's Ritual Chocolate. In 2023, Ritual teamed up with Caputo's to make a bar that might be the ultimate reminder that beauty can emerge from the sordid chaos of existence. It's made entirely with wild cacao from Volker Lehmann's Tranquilidad estate.

Yes, Volker's back. Although he walked away from chocolate in 2014, he couldn't stay away. He missed cacao, and he especially missed Tranquilidad, the one thing he'd managed to salvage from the bankruptcy lawyers.

So he came back with a promise to himself: no more scale, no more chasing the big score. He would just make what Tranquilidad could produce, a few tons at most, and he would make it all by hand. It would be the most perfect, fussed-over cacao in the world, and he would find a maker in the States who could do it justice.

That part, at least, has gone according to plan. Ritual and Caputo's found the sweet spot, a 75 percent cacao that intensifies the haunting tobacco and spice notes I'd fallen for in that first taste of Cru Sauvage fourteen years ago. One of the people who fell under its spell was Ari Weinzweig—the cofounder of Zingerman's, the specialty foods powerhouse—who added it to his catalog and raved about it in his popular newsletter. "The chocolate is truly exceptional," he wrote, "like listening to music for the first time on a radically better sound system."

The bar is the second offering in Caputo's Preservation Program series, after Luisa Abram's Juruá bar, with all proceeds going to the Heirloom Cacao Preservation Fund. In addition, Caputo's sends an extra dollar per bar directly to Volker to help him and his chocolatal survive.

That part is still a work in progress. Volker's new vision is to transform Tranquilidad into a combination field station and cacao camp where researchers, chocolate makers, and chocolate lovers can come to see wild cacao, learn how to work with it, and continue the movement. He began to build a guesthouse to welcome visitors, with the goal of having it ready for a blowout celebration of Tranquilidad's twentieth anniversary in late 2023. I was supposed to go, but in November he emailed to say that everything was on hold. "I write to you with some sadness, but also joy," he wrote. The party was off. "My pockets are pretty empty. I put so much in the buildings that I ran out of cash. The guesthouse is not ready and the dining room and kitchen are still with a leaking roof. The bats love it."

Volker hoped things would improve for 2024. In the meantime, his old Crocodile Cacao partner Stefan Bloch, who had been the first person to take a chance on his weird beans and show them to Felchlin, was coming for a short visit. "He brings Cru Sauvage and the new Tranquilidad bar," Volker wrote. "So we do a little memory tasting and see how this ends."

There in the little chocolate shop in New Hampshire, I raise the bowl to my mouth and drink. Dancing Lion is perhaps the only place in the world you can almost always find Tranquilidad chocolate. From four thousand miles away, I sip Bolivian rainforest, enjoying my fifteen seconds of tranquility, watching the bubbles of foam dance in and out of existence as the first flush of well-being seeps in. This is the nature of chocolate. The hut may be leaky, the bowl chipped, the heart broken. And still, there is the momentary ecstasy of this bittersweet offering.

ACKNOWLEDGMENTS

My journey down the rabbit hole of cacao might never have happened were it not for Clay Gordon and his wonderful website TheChocolateLife. I'd been writing about chocolate for years, and had read online reviews of Cru Sauvage and its mysterious mastermind, Volker Lehmann, but Clay's site was the first to include a forum where people from all over the chocolate world could converse. It was the only place to get real information about Volker and his beans, and he himself was weighing in (strongly, true to form) on a variety of issues. Clay confirmed that Volker was an interesting dude, and he was even planning a visit to Tranquilidad himself. We even thought about coordinating our trips, though the timing didn't work out. Now, fifteen years later, TheChocolateLife is still going strong, and Clay has continued to be an invaluable resource and a friend.

That first trip to Bolivia became a story for *Outside Magazine*. I thank my editors there, Jeremy Spencer and Chris Keyes, for taking the chance on a very unpredictable venture, and for helping shape it into an iconic *Outside* story. That was the beginning of an incredibly fruitful relationship that has led to some of my best work.

In Bolivia, Volker Lehmann went out of his way (twice!) to show me his world, to explain it, and to keep me more or less alive while doing so. He even fed me well. (The caiman ceviche was a showstopper.) Special thanks to the people of Baures,

Huacaraje, Combate, Camiaco, El Carmen, Bella Vista, and Trinidad for their warm hospitality.

It was Matt Caputo who first alerted me to Luisa Abram and Andre Banks and the amazing things they were doing in the Brazilian Amazon. Matt was generous with his knowledge and opinions and continues to be a driving force in the world of heirloom cacao.

In Brazil, Luisa and Andre and the rest of their family—Andrea, Miriam, and Fabio—were incredible hosts, giving me rich insights into Brazilian culture and experience. The Juruá communities of Rebojo and Novo Horizonte also rolled out the red carpet for us—even if it was covered in electric eels.

Those 2022 trips were done in collaboration with Kaleidoscope Content for our podcast series *Wild Chocolate*. I thank the amazing Mangesh Hattikudur for reaching out and agreeing to a plan that, again, was a huge roll of the dice. It all worked out, thanks to the superb skills and creativity of Mangesh, Shane McKeon, Kate Osborn, Spencer Stephenson, Casey Holford, Oz Woloshyn, and Constantinos Linos.

And frankly, a big part of why it worked out were the verbal dynamics of Mark Christian, whose knowledge of chocolate and way of talking about it holds no equal. Mark is god's gift to the interviewer. Just ask a question, press "Play," and sit back.

In Belize, I got to see two extraordinary cacao operations at work. I'm still amazed that Emily Stone let me sit in for every meeting and visit at Maya Mountain Cacao, and fielded every one of my questions with great thoughtfulness. At BFREE, Jacob Marlin regaled me with some of the most entertaining stories one could hope for, in one of the most magical settings, and Elmer Tzalam helped me understand what it takes to grow a cacao forest from scratch.

Over the years, many other people helped fill out the story of chocolate for me, including Julio Saqui, Alex Whitmore, Colin Gasko, Dan O'Doherty, Diane Coy, and Richard Tango-Lowy, whose Dancing Lion Chocolate showed me the heights to which chocolate could ascend in the hands of a master.

And speaking of masters, my journeys with the Heirloom Cacao Preservation Fund in Mexico and Guatemala introduced me to many, who were extremely generous with their expertise. Thank you to Carlos Eichenberger, Ana Rita García Lascuraín, Mónica Lozano, Daniel Reza, Carina Santiago, Olga Cabrera, Flor Heras, Shava Cueva, Dionisia Garcia Juárez, Alma Delia Magaña Peralta, Pablo Muguerza, Carlos Avendaño Arrazate, Alexander Mendoza López, and Ajax Moreno. Those expeditions were expertly led by Alejandro Zamorano and Erick Ac, and they benefited from the planning and support of the HCP leadership team of Alyssa D'Adamo, Anne Zaczek, Jody Hayden, and Jacob Marlin.

For this all to become a book took the enthusiastic support of my agent, Angela Miller, and my editors at Bloomsbury, Harriet LeFavour and Nancy Miller. And most important of all, the home-front support of Mary Elder Jacobsen, who kept the lights on and the dog upright while I slipped off to the tropics for one last bit of research.

RESOURCES

MAIL-ORDER CHOCOLATE

CAPUTO'S

caputos.com

One-stop shopping that includes most of the world's best bars, from the top importer in the United States. Check out the bars made under Caputo's Preservation Program, which partners with great producers to pull off nearly impossible projects and outfits them in museum-grade packaging. So far there are three, all featured in this book: Luisa Abram's Juruá bar, Volker Lehmann's Tranquilidad, and Jacob Marlin's wild Criollo from BFREE.

DANCING LION CHOCOLATE

dancinglion.us/cacao

I've never liked the "Queen of Versailles" aesthetic that has always dominated the chocolate world. Dancing Lion fixes that with something much more sophisticated, understated, and trippy. It's also one of the only chocolatiers in the country to make its own chocolate, forging bonbons and bars and "edible art" out of the world's best beans, often using different sources for each piece of the puzzle, to layered effect. Best drinking chocolate I know.

THE MEADOW

themeadow.com

Extraordinarily well-curated chocolate shops in New York City and Portland, Oregon, with an equally indulgent selection online.

Rather than work with national distributors, the Meadow specializes in direct relationships with small producers.

CHOCOLATE-MAKING SUPPLIES

CHOCOLATE ALCHEMY

chocolatealchemy.com

John Nanci launched the home-chocolatier revolution in 2004 with his site Chocolate Alchemy, which for the first time put the tools for making bean-to-bar chocolate into the hands of every cocoa-curious amateur, and it's still the go-to site for tabletop chocolate making. Beans, nibs, equipment, instructions, and philosophy, all under one URL.

CLASSES

ECOLE CHOCOLAT

ecolechocolat.com

Since 2003, the destination for chocolate learning of all kinds, for aspiring amateurs and professionals alike. Most classes are taught online, until you get really, really serious.

INFORMATION

THE C-SPOT

c-spot.com

Mark Christian's quirky and erudite website, filled with entertaining reviews and in-depth dives into chocolate history, science, and lore.

THECHOCOLATELIFE
thechocolatelife.com
The original website devoted to chocolate (like, way back when the Web was young) and still the most comprehensive, this is a full-blown community forum with thousands of members, ongoing discussions, classified listings, and weekly livestreams with founder Clay Gordon and special guests.

DAME CACAO
damecacao.com
Great chocolate blog from world traveler Max Gandy, with gobs of information about every aspect of the world of chocolate. Especially thoughtful on environmental and social justice issues.

FINE CHOCOLATE INDUSTRY ASSOCIATION
finechocolateindustry.org
For the pros! News, events, webinars, schmoozing, and more.

HEIRLOOM CACAO PRESERVATION FUND
hcpcacao.org
Posts, videos, and educational resources about heirloom cacao and the quest to preserve it. Includes a full list of HCP designees and chronicles of HCP's expeditions in search of more undiscovered masterpieces.

FESTIVALS

CAPUTO'S ANNUAL CHOCOLATE FESTIVAL
caputos.com/chocfest
A gathering of Salt Lake City's finest chefs, mixologists, and chocolate makers, with all proceeds benefiting the Heirloom Cacao Preservation Fund.

NORTHWEST CHOCOLATE FESTIVAL

nwchocolate.com

If you care about artisan chocolate, this is the one you want to go to. A two-day blowout in Washington State each fall, with everything you'd expect from an industry conference: awards, demos, seminars, tastings, workshops, and thousands of exhibitors.

INDEX

Note: Page numbers in *italics* denote images and associated captions.

A NOTE ON THE AUTHOR

ROWAN JACOBSEN is the author of the James Beard Award–winning *A Geography of Oysters* as well as *American Terroir*, *Apples of Uncommon Character*, *Truffle Hound*, and other books. His books have been named to numerous top ten lists, and he has been featured on *All Things Considered*, *The Splendid Table*, *Morning Edition*, and *CBS This Morning* and in the pages of *Bon Appétit*, *Saveur*, the *Wall Street Journal*, the *Washington Post*, and elsewhere. He lives in Vermont.